MIND SPACE

AND

TIME STREAM

ALSO BY RALPH METZNER

Alchemical Divination (2009)

The Roots of War and Domination (2008)

The Expansion of Consiousness (2008)

Sacred Vine of Spirits – Ayahuasca (ed., 2006)

Sacred Mushroom of Visions – Teonanácatl (ed., 2005)

Green Psychology (1999)

The Unfolding Self (1998)

The Well of Remembrance (1994)

Through the Gateway of the Heart (ed., 1985)

Know Your Type (1979)

Maps of Consciousness (1971)

The Ecstatic Adventure (ed., 1968)

The Psychedelic Experience (1964; with Timothy Leary and Richard Alpert)

MIND SPACE

AND

TIME STREAM

Understanding and Navigating
Your States of Consciousness

by
Ralph Metzner

Green Earth Foundation
&
Regent Press

Copyright © 2009 by Ralph Metzner

All rights reserved.

ISBN 13: 978-1-58790-172-0
ISBN 10: 1-58790-172-2
Library of Congress Control Number: 2009936308

Graphics & Layout by Cynthia Smith
Cover Photo by Ralph Metzner

Published by
REGENT PRESS
www.regentpress.net

for

GREEN EARTH FOUNDATION
www.greenearthfound.org

Printed in the U.S.A.
REGENT PRESS
2747 Regent Street
Berkeley, CA 94705
e-mail: regentpress@mindspring.com

Printed on 30% post-consumer recycled fiber,
archival [acid free] paper

Contents

Preface i

1 Altered States 1
2 Consciousness, Space and Time 7
3 Consciousness as Context and Subjectivity. 13
4 Radical Empiricism 25
5 States, Stages and Levels of Consciousness 31
6 The Set and Setting Model. 41
7 Waking, Sleeping, Dreaming, Meditating. 49
8 The Dimensions of Energy and Pleasure/Pain 63
9 Expansions of Consciousness 73
10 Contractions of Consciousness. 83
11 Dissociation and State Transitions 95
12 Association and Dissociation in Various States 107
13 NDE, OBE and Mediumistic States. 115

Appendix A: The Altered State Graphic Profile 129
Appendix B: Neurochemical Correlates of the Two Dimensions 132
Appendix C: Dissociative Drug States 137
Appendix D: Biochemical and Hormonal Basis of Sexual Experience ... 139

References and Select Bibliography 141

Preface

In this book I propose to relate my distillation of almost five decades of research, psychotherapy, shamanic and yogic practices, as well as teaching experience, on the role of changing states of consciousness in psychological health and spiritual growth. My interest in this area was sparked in the early 1960s, when, as a graduate student, I collaborated with Timothy Leary, Richard Alpert and others in the Harvard research projects on what we called "consciousness expanding" substances.

At that time psychology in the Harvard Graduate School of Social Relations was dominated by the two radically different paradigms of behaviorism and psychoanalysis – so different that the strict Skinnerian behaviorists even had a separate building, where they ran their experiments on schedules of reinforcement in pigeons and rats. In accord with the integrative approach of the Social Relations programs, we studied how Freudian ideas were being applied outside the framework of individual psychoanalytic therapy, e. g. in cultural anthropology. I appreciated the integrative approach: my first published paper in an academic journal applied findings from animal learning studies to better understand human learning in neurosis and in psychotherapy.

In that academic environment, drug-induced experiences of "expanded consciousness" were like an intellectual bombshell. Harvard faculty and administrators reacted with alarm and disapproval to the approach Leary espoused – which was for the researchers to first have the experience themselves before giving it to others. He pointed out that a strict behaviorist approach to these states was absurd – there was no behavior to observe, as the subject might lie silently for hours, with only an occasional "whew" of amazement. On the other hand, psychoanalysis also could not offer any understanding of these unusual states. The psychoanalyst I was seeing for my personal analysis involving dreams and the like, told me without judgment (to his credit) that he did not know what to make of the experiences I was describing.

Although the works of C. G. Jung were not on the curriculum at the Harvard Department of Social Relations, it wasn't until we started reading Jung and his explorations of Eastern wisdom traditions, like Tibetan Buddhism and Yoga, that we began to find conceptual maps and deeper understanding of the spiritual dimensions of psychedelic experience. Following a suggestion of Aldous Huxley, we adapted the Tibetan Book of the Dead as a manual for psychedelic experiences – where "dying" was seen as analogous to relinquishing egoic self-images, and "rebirth" as re-entry to the consciousness of ordinary existence. My interest in Eastern philosophies, worldviews and practices has remained a constant throughout my life: for years I taught courses comparing Eastern and Western teachings concerning consciousness and self.

Leary's most important contribution to the theoretical understanding of states of consciousness was what came to be known as the set-and-setting hypothesis, according to which the content of a psychedelic experience could only be understood by considering the set or intention, as well as the setting or context. The drug, according to this view, acted as a kind of non-specific catalyst, propelling the individual into another state of consciousness. This is the feature that sets psychedelic drugs apart from any other drug known to medicine: they do not affect liver or heart or muscular function, they affect the brain and thus the very means of our perception and interpretations of reality. Later, in my courses on states of consciousness at CIIS, I came to apply this set-and-setting model, which I discuss in chapter 6 of this book, to all states of consciousness, including the ordinary waking state, dreams, meditation, hypnosis, etc.

Although Leary certainly knew of William James, his illustrious predecessor as Harvard psychologist from a century before, I don't recall him ever explicitly mentioning James's principle of radical empiricism. But Leary was, like James, a proponent of the scientific, empirical approach to gathering knowledge – and of extending this approach (contrary to Behaviorism) to our knowledge of interior states. Thus, our initial research studies focused on gathering questionnaire and interview data from subjects who had these experiences and analyzing them in the light of the set-and-setting theory. I describe and discuss William James epistemology of radical empiricism in chapter 4.

After completing my Ph. D. in clinical psychology at Harvard (for which I was not permitted to do research on the already taboo subject of psychedelics) I obtained a one-year post-doctoral fellowship to study pharmacology at the Harvard Medical School. I immersed myself in the technical literature on the biochemistry and neurophysiology of psychoactive drugs – which has remained a life-long interest. In the course of my life I have edited four books in which accounts of the subjective experiences with psychoactive plant-drugs are combined with surveys of the objective scientific knowledge (both biological and cultural) about these substances: *The Ecstatic Adventure* (LSD), *Through the Gateway of the Heart* (MDMA), *Sacred Vine of Spirits –Ayahuasca,* and *Sacred Mushroom of Visions – Teonanácatl.* In the present book, I describe findings and theories on the neurochemical bases of states of consciousness in Appendix B.

Before coming to the Harvard Graduate School of Social Relations, I had spent my undergraduate years at The Queen's College, Oxford University, where I studied philosophy (which was mainly Wittgensteinian linguistic analysis) and psychology (which was the experimental laboratory kind). My favorite philosophy professor at Oxford was John L. Austin, a master of dry wit, who advocated the analysis of the hidden philosophical assumptions in ordinary language, and tracing the etymological roots of words for clues to our perception of the world. I have practiced this approach and learned from it, my whole life. In chapters 2 and 3 of this book, I pursue some of the fascinating semantic associations of the concept of consciousness, particularly in relation to our notions of space and time. I resonate with the Buddhist teaching that consciousness or mind is like the space in which thoughts and sensations appear and disappear, again and again.

At the California Institute of Integral Studies (CIIS) I taught a course on Altered States of Consciousness for over 20 years, in which we discussed the common states we're all familiar with, as well as the unusual states of mysticism, or those induced by drugs, or yogic practices, or music, or movement, or any number of other catalysts and triggers. I tried very hard to normalize alterations of consciousness, wanting to disconnect the term "altered state" from implications of pathology. Only in the last ten years or so, I finally found what I believe to be the root of my (and others') discomfort with the term: "altered" implies something was done to you – contradicting the core insight on the centrality of set or intention. I have since that time stopped, or at least decreased, my use of the term "altered states." I relate the details of my semantic conversion experience on this term in chapter 1.

I still use the concept of state of consciousness, which is always defined by a period of time between two transitions. And I argue for clearly distinguishing this from the idea of levels of consciousness, which is a completely different paradigm: these levels are considered permanent structural features of our psyche and of the world. I elaborate on these paradigm differences in chapter 5; and also point out that there is a third paradigm – that of stages of consciousness development. In Western psychologies the development of consciousness in childhood and the entire life-cycle is a core theme. Eastern philosophies are more often concerned with stages of development associated with spiritual practices.

In chapter 7, I describe the four common states, familiar to everyone – waking, sleeping, dream and relaxation/meditation. Comparing Western research findings in the psychophysiology of these states with Yogic and Buddhist teachings (which also recognize four basic states), yields some fascinating convergences, as well as striking differences. The biggest difference is that in the West we assume we normally "have" consciousness," except when we're unconscious in sleep, anesthesia or coma. Yogic and Buddhist teachings insist that unconsciousness (*avidya*) is the default condition of the human being from birth on – and consciousness can only be developed or cultivated, through yogic and mindfulness practices, in every state of consciousness and in our lives in general.

In chapter 8, I present a conceptual framework for distinguishing common states in terms of two dimensions – the level

v

of energy or arousal, and the pleasure-pain spectrum. This model deals only with the subjective energy level and feeling-tone of the different states, and not with particular contents of thoughts, images and the like. The states induced by psychoactive stimulants and sedatives can be mapped on these dimensions – but not the psychedelics, because their actions are too varied and complex.

Expanded and expansive states, which I discuss in chapter 9, involve a broadening and deepening of the scope of attention and perception, such as occurs when we awaken. They may occur with psychedelic drugs; but can also occur with mystical practices, or be triggered spontaneously in the fire of creative inspiration, by a walk in an old growth forest, or by a soul-stirring musical performance.

Although the ability to contract or focus awareness is a normal and essential mental function, unconsciously contracted states involve a fixated narrowing of attention and perception. I discuss contracted states, of which the most familiar are states of fear and states of rage, in chapter 10. In more extreme and repetitive form, we recognize these contracted states in obsessions, compulsions and addictive behaviors.

In chapter 11, I discuss the elusive and ill-understood process of dissociation or disconnection – the opposite process of associative connection. Every state transition (e. g. waking up) involves a degree of dissociation from the previous state, as we enter into the mind-space and time-stream of the new state. Sometimes the switching from one state to another occurs unconsciously, and may involves different ego-states or multiple personas. Hypnotic trance, which involves a directed dissociation from ordinary reality, is often the only way that such split identities can be brought to consciously relate with one another. The relative preponderance of associative and dissociative processes varies in different states of consciousness – as I discuss in chapter 12. Recognizing them can contribute greatly to the healing of psychopathology and the deepening of psychospiritual growth.

In the final chapter 13, I discuss some relatively unfamiliar states of consciousness, involving a high degree of dissociation from ordinary reality – states that were quite unusual in the past, but which have been more widely reported in our times. Near-death experiences (NDE) occur when people have crossed over the threshold and returned, bringing astonishing messages from the hereafter. In out-of-body experiences (OBE) the person finds himself in a kind of double or subtle body, being able to fly around the ordinary time-space reality, and looking down on their physical form. In mediumistic states, also called channeling, some other being – deceased ancestor, angelic guide or ET – "comes through" and offers healings and teachings.

It is my hope that these reflections on various states of consciousness, both ordinary and extraordinary, may help awaken in the reader a greater sense of the vastness of human experience and of their evolutionary spiritual potentials.

* * *

1
Altered States

The concept of altered states of consciousness (ASCs) came into prominence in Western psychology in the 1950s and 1960s, primarily due to three paradigm breakthroughs. One was the discovery of rapid eye movements (REM) during dreaming sleep, which was the first time recordable physiological variations could be reliably correlated with a specific subjective state of consciousness. The second breakthrough was the discovery that recordings of electrical activity in the brain (EEG), in the frequency range of 8-12 cycles per second (called "alpha waves") were reliably correlated with calm, eyes-closed states of relaxation and meditation. The third breakthrough was the discovery of LSD and other psychedelic, consciousness expanding drugs, – which meant that profoundly transformed and transformative states of consciousness, hitherto accessible only to a few individuals engaged in meditative or yogic practices, could be induced with fairly high reliability in ordinary people, given the right preparation, safeguards and set and setting.

These discoveries of correlations between variations in neural functions and variations in subjective consciousness stimulated an enormous upsurge of research, which continues to this day, using technologies such EEG, MRI, PET and others. This approach – the study of associations between measures of brain activity and mental states – has become the dominant paradigm in the scientific study of consciousness. It is based on the underlying philosophical assumption of the Western, materialist worldview that consciousness must somehow **be located in the brain.** This is a view that goes back to the work of the 18th century French mathematician René Descartes, who famously speculated that **the soul might be found in the pineal gland.** The Eastern philosophies of Yoga and Buddhism come from a completely different approach, basing their conceptions of the mind on systematic observations of inner states during meditation.

The key insight that came out of the Harvard studies with psychedelic drugs in the 1960s, was the significance of set (intention) and setting (context) in understanding psychedelic states of consciousness. Unlike drugs that affect the functioning of one or another bodily organ, psychedelics expand the range, focus and clarity of perception itself – the way we see reality and ourselves.

Timothy Leary used to say psychedelic drugs were potentially to psychology what the microscope was to biology and the telescope to astronomy – affording the conscious perception of ranges and levels of reality that were previously inaccessible. But just as what we perceive through a microscope is a function of what we have put on the slide (such as the leaf of a plant, or a drop of blood), so the content of a psychedelic experience (the thoughts, images, feelings, sensations) is a function of the pre-existing **set or intention, and the chosen context or setting.** The drug merely functions as a kind of catalyst and amplifier of perception.

In the graduate courses on altered states of consciousness that I taught for many years, I found it useful to expand this basic paradigm of set, setting and catalyst to any and all states of consciousness, from the most common to the most exotic. Well-known catalysts or triggers of ASCs (besides drugs) are hypnotic inductions, meditative practices, shamanic drumming, music, nature, sex, and others, as well as the normal cyclical variations of brain chemistry that catalyze us into the sleeping or waking states. It's also useful to apply the ASC paradigm to understand psycho-pathological states that are contractive, fixated or dissociative, and have negative and toxic consequences for individuals, families and communities – including drug or behavioral addictions, fear (panic attacks), rage (fits of temper), psychotic breaks or episodes, depression, mania and others. We shall discuss such states in a later chapter.

One issue that produces uneasiness in most people when considering or discussing the concept of an "altered state," is the seeming implication that "altered" is itself abnormal. How then could we talk about ASCs being therapeutic, creative, or spiritual growth enhancing? In my courses, I've attempted to overcome this cognitive prejudice by pointing to the fact that all human beings are very familiar with the normal, profoundly altered variations in state we call sleeping, waking and dreaming. Sigmund Freud had said that dreams are the "royal road to the unconscious," meaning they provide the broadest and widest access. But one could equally well say that dreams are the commoners' road, for everyone can and does travel on that nightly passage into the realms beyond. In India the "royal path of yoga" (*raja yoga*) referred to the intentional use of psychological practices to liberate consciousness from its ordinary conditioning – and this path does require a certain disciplined study and application.

Some writers have attempted to overcome the negative presuppositions associated with the concept of "altered states," by proposing terms such as "alternate state," or "non-ordinary state," or (as in a recently published handbook of the American Psychological Association) "anomalous experiences." But this linguistic strategy disguises the point that some alterations of state are extremely ordinary, usual and familiar. Should "dreaming" be considered a non-ordinary state? How about being "drunk" or "depressed" – aren't those rather ordinary, all-too familiar states? Furthermore, some indigenous people and shamanic practitioners object that what Westerners called "non-ordinary" states or realities, are to them very familiar and ordinary. There is a whole spectrum of states of consciousness, from the familiar and common to the anomalous and exotic extreme. Whether the state is normal or abnormal is, in any case, a culturally and historically relative judgment imposed on experience, and thus, an academic question of no particular significance.

I finally came to understand my own lingering discomfort with the concept of "altered state," besides the fact that it confuses the distinction between ordinary and non-ordinary states: it has to do with the passive construction "altered," which suggests that something was done to you by an external agency. A drug-induced state seemingly supports this view. But we have to remember that normally the individual chooses to ingest the drug, whether alcohol or LSD or marijuana, for a certain purpose, and with the intention to alter their own consciousness. Similarly, a person may choose to undergo a hypnotic induction procedure to enter into a trance state in the context of psychotherapy. To deliberately alter another person's consciousness without their knowledge or consent, for example by surreptitious use of a drug or alcohol, is universally considered morally reprehensible and illegal.

The state transitions of everyday life can also be conceived, and experienced, in active or passive terms. We may "go to sleep" with the conscious intention toward rest and restoration of energies, we may "fall asleep" involuntarily due to fatigue, or we may be "put to sleep," metaphorically and literally, by a boring speaker in a lecture hall. Likewise for the opposite transition: we may "be awakened" by the alarm clock; just "wake up" spontaneously; or struggle, literally and metaphorically, against the downward pull of somnolence, to become more fully conscious and alert.

In Buddhism and other spiritual traditions, such as those of Gurdjieff, what we consider our normal waking state is seen as a kind of sleep state, in which we are unconscious of our essential nature. According to such teachings, the purpose of yogic and meditative practices is to help us awaken from the somnolent, dream-like conditions of ordinary, non-conscious existence – and awaken to our highest spiritual and creative potentials.

In order to use expansive, positive states of consciousness constructively for increasing health, creativity and growth, we need to be able to recognize the state we're in at any given time, and how to navigate through it. In shamanic and alchemical divination practices, *sonic driving* methods such as drumming or rattling are used to facilitate accessing knowledge for healing, problem solving and guidance. Yogis and meditators practice mindfulness and concentration methods in order to experience the subtler dimensions of consciousness.

With contractive and unhealthy states, such as fear and rage, we need to identify the state we're in, and recognize how it's affecting us (our thinking, our perception, our behavior), as well as others with whom we may be relating. We need to learn how to navigate our way through the negative states and into healthier, life-affirming states. By becoming more conscious of the state we're in at any given moment, we can deploy attention in different ways, enhance the range of choices we can make, and more fully take responsibility for the impact of those choices on others and in our world.

* * *

2
Consciousness, Space and Time

The word "consciousness" has a variety of meanings in everyday usage and these meanings are complicated by the various and vigorously debated theories of consciousness in the philosophy of mind, in epistemology, psychology, religion and anthropology. Derived from Latin *con* – "with" and *scire* – "to know," the etymology suggests knowledge shared or communicated between persons. On the other hand, we have the commonly held conception of consciousness as purely private, subjective experience. The notion that consciousness is somehow an interpersonal or social construction can be found in such concepts as "tribal consciousness," or "mass-mind," or "collective unconscious." It is implicit as well in group processes of "consciousness raising," as practiced in certain feminist activist groups.

There is an intriguing and meaningful affinity of "consciousness" with "conscience." Both words are derived from the same linguistic root, though they have different connotations. Whereas "consciousness" is seemingly morally neutral, "conscience" has a moral dimension: it is not only knowledge of right and wrong, it implies an internalized motivation or imperative to "do the right thing." In some languages one word covers both concepts – in French *la conscience*, in Spanish *la conciencia*; whereas in German (*Bewusstsein, Gewissen*) and Italian (*conoszenza, conszienza*) the two terms betray their related meaning. The semantic affinity of these concepts points to an important psychic fact: that when we become more conscious, or heighten awareness, we are thereby more in touch with our inner spiritual values and thus more likely to make morally appropriate choices.

Some use "consciousness" as synonymous with "awareness" in the sense of sensory perception of internal or external states and conditions. Thus we say someone is "unconscious" if they seem not to be perceiving or reacting to perceptual stimuli such as sights, sounds, etc. Others use "awareness" for simple, immediate sense experience; and "consciousness" for organized, complexes of perception, feeling and knowledge. This distinction enables us to talk about unconscious perceptions and bringing unconscious feelings to conscious awareness.

The relationship of consciousness to self-perception is mysterious and elusive: becoming conscious of different aspects of one's self is seen in psychology as a positive, healthy development, whereas being "self-conscious" is an excessive focus on self that is socially debilitating. Furthermore, many spiritual traditions teach that spiritual growth is a function of the degree to which we are able to transcend the ego or self, or even suppress or do away with it. We shall return to this issue in chapter 11.

Historically, there have been two main metaphors for consciousness, one *spatial* or *topographical*, and the other *temporal* or *developmental*. The topographical metaphor is expressed in conceptions of consciousness as like a terrain, or a field, or a state – one can enter into it and come out of it. We travel and explore inner space, or mind-space, in our shamanic journeys, our dreams and meditations.

The spatial metaphor for consciousness is also implicit in the

Buddhist conception of consciousness like empty space (*sunyata*). One of the key practices in Buddhist meditation is to contemplate the identity of form (*rupa*) and emptiness (*sunyata*)." Form is emptiness and emptiness is not different from form," according to the *Heart Sutra*. Meditating on emptiness is the preparatory phase for the elaborate visualizations of the Buddhist *tantras*.

A somewhat analogous Western practice that grew out of brain-wave biofeedback research is Lester Fehmi's *Open Focus* method of progressively focusing on the space *between* structures of the body – the space between the ears, between the shoulders, between the hips, etc and visualizing body cavities like the head, the thorax, the abdomen as filled with empty space. This practice tends to produce synchronous alpha waves in the EEG and a relaxed feeling of subjective spaciousness.

A temporal metaphor for consciousness, seen as a succession of events in time, with duration and transition, is implicit in conceptions such as William James' stream of thought, or the stream of awareness, the flow of experience. Historically, we see the temporal metaphor emphasized in the thought of the pre-Socratic philosophers Thales and Heraclitus.

Buddhist teachings of impermanence (*anicca*), and the Taoist emphasis on the flows and eddies of water as the basic patterns of all life also exemplify the temporal metaphor. From this point of view, wave-like fluctuations of consciousness are regarded as natural and inevitable. Health, well-being and creativity are linked to one's ability to tune into and utilize the naturally occurring, and the "artificially" induced, modulations of consciousness.

I suggest that the most balanced way to think about consciousness is to keep both the spatial and the temporal perspectives in mind. We can recognize and identify the structural, persistent features of the world and the state we are "in" at any given moment; *and* we can be aware of the ever-changing, flowing stream of phenomena in which we are immersed. "We cannot step twice into the same river," is an oft-quoted aphorism of the enigmatic hermit philosopher Heraclitus. But the quote is incomplete – his actual statement was more profound: "Though we stand in the same river, the flowing water is always different." This statement accords well with a dual perspective that recognizes both the spatial dimensions and the temporal fluidity of our experience, both mind-space and time-stream.

In the indigenous, shamanistic traditions there exists the practice of the shamanic journey, whether induced by psychoactive plants or rhythmic drumming. The "journey" is the preferred indigenous way of talking about an experience of moving in and through a particular state of consciousness. The shaman's body is lying on the ground motionless, while his spirit, or his soul, or awareness, is travelling or moving through inner space (or "non-ordinary reality"). After the journey, there is a "return" to ordinary reality, to home and family, bringing back healing knowledge and visionary power.

The definition of consciousness proposed by the Russian mathematician and physicist Victor Nalimov, in his book *Realms of the Human Unconscious,* is also one that integrates both the topographical and the temporal aspect: he calls it a "semantic continuum," i. e. a continuum of meaning. A continuum of meaning, like the sensorium of sense perception, conveys something of the dual quality of consciousness, - both stable and fluid, both integrative and differentiated. Some findings from the scientific study of brain function suggest that these two aspects of consciousness may be correlated with differential activity in the two hemisphere: the left brain, with the language centers, is more associated with temporal, linear processing; and the right brain, active in perception of design and shape, with spatial awareness.

Whether we are on an external journey, or experiencing a particular state of consciousness, we're moving through spaces and places, inner and outer, guided by our intentions and questions. Our journeys, whether external or internal, inevitably have a certain duration and sequence in time, they "take time," as we say. Einsteinian relativity theory tells us of a *continuum of space-time* or *time-space*. And so it is in inner space explorations as well: we are always moving along a time-line, or time-stream, tracking past developments in memory, or future possibilities in vision. When we disconnect from the time-space dimensions of consensus waking-state reality, we enter into a different state or space that has its own characteristic time-line or time-stream.

✷ ✷ ✷

3
Consciousness as Context and Subjectivity

The etymology of the word "consciousness" (*con-scire*, "with-knowing") implies a relational, or systems view, as discussed in the last chapter – pointing to the relation between subject and object. Conscious knowing is knowing with knowing-that-you-know. Are there forms of knowing that are not conscious, in this sense? Certainly, there is unconscious knowing involved in our knowing how to grow hair, or skin cells over a wound, and other "autonomic" physiological functions of the body. Then there are the forms of knowing – such as how to tie shoelaces, or how to ride a bicycle – that initially required conscious practice, but have become automated habits, involving non-conscious knowing. The proportion of conscious functioning to unconsciousness is (obviously) difficult to assess – like the proverbial tip of the iceberg. Eric Kandel, a Nobel laureate neuroscientist, has estimated that

> Eighty to 90 percent of what we do is unconscious. When we speak, we use presumably correct grammatical structures while paying little if any conscious attention to this grammar. And we act in lots of other ways without having the slightest clue what we are actually doing. (*Scientific American Mind*, Oct/Nov 2008, p. 16)

The conclusions of modern brain science in this regard are more in accord with Eastern and esoteric teachings about the nature of consciousness than they support the conventional assumptions of the Western worldview. In Western culture, we tend to assume that, ordinarily, we are conscious, or we "have consciousness." We do recognize that there are unconscious states, such as sleep, or coma; and we also have come to recognize, since the writings of Sigmund Freud, that unconscious impulses, thoughts and feelings can have a profound influence on our normal, waking state consciousness. Eastern psychologies, on the other hand, including those of Vedanta and Buddhism, regard unconsciousness (called *avidya*, "not-knowing") as the default condition of the human being, from birth on; and consciousness as something that is generated – like an additional perception of a web of connections.

Consciousness, according to those teachings, only develops as a result of disciplined mental and psychological practices known as meditation and the different forms of yoga. Such was also the view of the teachings of G. I. Gurdjieff, who insisted that humans, when functioning in the ordinary waking state, are actually asleep and functioning like automata. Only through mindfulness practice, or what he called "self-remembering," could one hope to generate consciousness i. e. conscious thinking, perceiving, feeling and acting.

Following this line of thought, we can distinguish ordinary unconscious psychic functioning, from the same function exercised consciously, with added awareness and perception of context. I show these comparisons in the following table.

Ordinary habitual function	Conscious function, with context
perception	apperception
sympathy	empathy
knowledge or information	wisdom or understanding
reaction	response
orientation	attention
expectation, impulse, desire	intention or interest
sensing	clairsentience
habitual thinking	mindful thinking
dreaming	lucid dreaming
judgment	discernment

Perception and apperception. Perception plus awareness of emotional and associational context is apperception. In the *Thematic Apperception Test (TAT)*, invented by Henry A. Murray (who was one of my professors at Harvard University), you are shown ambiguous drawings of figures in various relational postures toward each other – and you write a story about "what is happening" in the picture. The story you tell reveals the thoughts, images and feelings that you are projecting in to the imaginary scene. The concept of apperception is in many ways applicable to psychedelic forms of expanded consciousness. Anyone who has had an experience with one of the classic hallucinogens (such as LSD, psilocybin or mescaline) knows that in such states you are not hallucinating in the sense of seeing something that isn't there, but rather you are perceiving more of what is there – clouds or webs of multiple mental, imagistic or emotional associations are being evoked, dependent of course on the perceiver's intentional set and personality.

Sympathy and empathy. In sympathy we resonate automatically and unconsciously with someone else's emotional state. Empathy, or compassion, also has that affective resonance – but in addition, there is an understanding of the situational context and the causes of the feelings. Sympathy is like you walk down the street and see someone in a hole, and you climb into it with them. "Misery loves company" is an apt motto for this reaction. Empathy implies more: you recognize the one in the hole and reach down with a helping hand. With sympathy you just feel as the other feels. This can be a totally unconscious reaction – like feeling depressed just by passing nearby to a depressed person in the street (without recognizing the connection). With empathy there is, in addition, recognition that you are not that person, though you feel some of the same feelings as the other. Empathy and the expression of it is a key factor in successful interpersonal conflict resolution and in psychotherapy. The substance MDMA has been called "empathogenic" for its ability to facilitate empathic connection in psychotherapy. The practice of *compassion*, its equivalent, plays a central role in Buddhist and other spiritual traditions.

Knowledge and understanding. The distinction between knowledge-about something, or information, (typically book-knowledge) on the one hand, and wisdom or understanding, which includes awareness of background and context, has often been drawn. Some like to make the same distinction by referring to it as "head-knowledge" vs "heart-knowledge." A person may know a lot about a certain subject matter, and be able to identify and describe relevant words and concepts – and yet not have the practical uses and applications of that knowledge. The latter requires wisdom and understanding – having experienced the truth of that knowledge and being able to "stand on" what one knows in practical terms.

Reaction and response. A reaction to a stimulus situation is immediate and instinctive, as in a child's or an animal's – "I want it" or "I hate it." A response, on the other hand, involves an ability to delay immediate gratification in the interests of adjusting to reality: it implies an element of forethought, planning and choice – a "response-ability". The ability to respond to situations appropriately, mediating between one's wishes of impulses and the objective facts of the situation, is called "reality testing," or also "time-binding" and is one of the hallmarks of civilized, mature, ethical conduct. Studies of brain development have concluded that the ability to anticipate future consequences of one's actions is related to the forebrain cortex, which does not completely hook up with the other, older parts of the brain until the mid- to late twenties.

Orientation and attention. Even relatively simple organisms have an orienting reflex – often a startle response, as when we, like any mammal, turn our heads toward a source of sudden loud sounds or towards vivid visual stimuli. The gesture of orienting sets the direction of attention – our attention is captured or captivated by intense or attractive stimuli. But we can also consciously and intentionally choose to direct our attention towards something. "My experience is what I choose to attend to," as William James said. In an interpersonal conversation or dialogue situation we attend by looking at and listening to our interlocutor. In mindfulness meditation, we choose to direct our attention inwardly, toward the breath or observing the never-ending **stream of thoughts**. The notion of attention implies something that is consciously chosen and extended: we "pay attention." In German, one says *wir schencken die Aufmerksamkeit* ("we give

17

attention"). Whether as a payment or a gift, the principle of attention as a conscious action is clear.

Expectation and intention. Words like "expectation," or "impulse," or "desire" refer to the directional vector of attention when it is unconscious. "We see what we want (or expect) to see" is a widely understood colloquial expression of this principle. Intent, interest, intentionality or set refer to the internal factors, consciously chosen, that determine the direction or focus of our attention. In the Harvard psychedelic research projects we observed that "set and setting" were the crucial determinants of the contents of a psychedelic state. But the "set-and-setting" hypothesis, as it came to be known, really applies to any state of consciousness – hypnosis, meditation, dreams, or what we call the ordinary, waking state of consensus reality. Your experience of the reading of this book, and mine in the writing of it, is to a large degree a function of the set or intention you and I bring to this communicative exchange, as well as the context or setting of the experience. The formula below, from my book *Alchemical Divination*, summarizes the relationships between intention, attention and awareness.

$$\left.\begin{array}{c}\textit{intention}\\\textit{or}\\\textit{question}\end{array}\right\} \longrightarrow \textit{attention} \longrightarrow \textit{awareness}$$

Sensing, seeing and hearing have their extended, more conscious forms – in *clairsentience, clairvoyance and clairaudience.* Yogic texts speak of such forms of extended, "clear" perception as *siddhis* ("attainments"). In Patanjali's *Yoga Sutras,* it is said that such *siddhis* may occur as result of birth (i. e. congenital); or through the use of certain herbs (i. e. psychoactive); or as a result of practices of mantra and disciplined concentration; or through the practice of deep meditative trance states (*samadhi*). With clairvoyant visual perception, whether occurring spontaneously or in a psychedelic or a meditative state, we see the object that we would ordinarily see, and in addition the subtler energetic frequencies – what some might call the "aura" of objects and living beings. "If the doors of perception were cleansed, everything would appear as it is – Infinite," as William Blake wrote in a famous verse. With clairaudient hearing we're hearing the subtle shadings of timbre and the harmonic overtones and undertones in music. With clairsentience, a skillful body-worker can sense the emotional-physical tension patterns in the body s/he is touching, and be able direct healing energy to resolve them.

Conditioned thinking and mindful thinking. Conditioned or habitual thinking tends to follow along well-trodden paths in our minds, like the routines we follow in our habitual working attitude. On the other hand, thinking consciously and intentionally along new associative pathways, "out-of-the-box" as we say, is one of the hallmarks of creativity. Witnessing one's own habitual thought processes, and how they are distorted by conditioned emotional reactions of fear and craving, is a key insight that **is gained through mindfulness meditation.** The mental and psychological practices of yoga aim at liberating the mind from its exclusive focus on the satisfaction of wants, what some call the "desire-mind," and learning to direct our thought processes according to conscious intention.

Dreaming and lucid dreaming. In ordinary dreams, there is a sequence of thoughts and images, often associated with feelings, sometimes body sensations, over which we have no conscious control. In lucid dreaming, which can be developed through yogic practices and meditation, the dreamer is conscious of the fact that he/she is in the dream state of consciousness. Becoming conscious, one can direct one's observations and actions in the dream according to interest or intention. And because the dreamer is in another, or "subtle" body, distinctly different from the physical, movements are possible, such as flying, that are impossible in ordinary time-space reality.

Automatic judgment and conscious discernment. In the course of our daily experience, our thoughts, images, feelings, perceptions and sensations are subject to immediate, mostly unconscious, reflexive evaluation. Sensations are judged pleasurable or painful; visual or auditory perceptions or images are beautiful or ugly; our feelings are good or bad; our motives and actions right or wrong; our thoughts true or false. The judgmental overlay over our experience is usually dichotomous, though in some situations a third possibility of indifference ("take it or leave it") may occur.

According to Paul MacLean's triune brain theory, basic feeling judgments of "approach versus avoid" are made in the limbic system, particularly the amygdala, and take precedence in time over higher brain-functions. It makes sense from an evolutionary point of view, that the capacity to judge potential threats should have priority access to our sensory-motor system. If I step off the curb to cross the street and see a moving object coming towards me, I jump back to avoid the danger – I don't take time to identify the nature of the beast or vehicle coming towards me.

Since the dichotomous judgment is superimposed on the perception, feeling, action or thought, prior to understanding – we can appropriately refer to it as "pre-judgment" or prejudice. Our perceptual prejudices restrict and block differentiated perception and crudely simplify our aesthetic and affective responses. "I don't know much about art, but I know what I like," conveys this attitude. In interpersonal relations, when blaming judgments and accusations intervene, communication ends. In one ayahuasca experience I had, the little green elves that I often see with this plant-teacher, said to me (somehow) – "you humans are really weird, you see everything in black and white, when there are really seven colors."

The prejudicial judgments we tend to impose on our experience restrict and limit our perception and understanding, but this is not to say that the capacity for judgments, for making choices for or against something or someone, is to be eliminated (even if such a thing were possible). When the judgments we make are accompanied by conscious observations, reflection and consideration of context, we are practicing "discernment," implying a heightened degree of differentiated awareness and situational **consideration**. The Buddhists call this quality "discriminative wisdom" – and it is one of the six *paramitas*, perfections or ideal qualities to be developed on the spiritual path.

Objective and Subjective Knowing

In the comparisons shown in the above table, the conscious function involves heightened perception and a constellation of associations. A systems view of humans and universe is implied here, a relational view of multi-level interconnectedness. In such a living systems worldview, the conscious communion of living subjects is acknowledged as equally real and valid as the conscious perception of identifiable objects. Things, objects and persons are temporary nodes in the web of life, in ever-changing patterned **relations** with other nodes. All being is interbeing, in Thich Nhat

Hanh's felicitous phrase.

Consciousness is the experiential side, the subjective knowing, feeling, sensing, imaging of relations, the "knowing-with," knowing from the inside point of view. This may be distinguished from the outside point of view, where we make observations about phenomena and communicate with other observers to develop a consensual description. A subjective experience communicated to and recognized by at least one other person becomes an objective observation. Hence: *subjective + 1 = objective*.

For example, scientists study a tree with objective measurements and analysis of its chemistry, botany, growth patterns, life-cycle, and so forth. As individuals, we can read and learn the categorized information about the tree – gathering what we call consensual, objective knowledge. Alternatively, we may merge in subjective empathy with the tree, so that we feel ourselves at one with it — experiencing the slow vegetative growth of trunk and branches, and possibly (if our worldview permits it) communing with the spirit of the tree.

One time, on a walk through a wooded area on Mt. Tamalpais, near where I live in Northern California, I was thinking to myself (with some frustration) that I didn't "know" many of the trees among which I was walking, i.e. I didn't know their botanical names. In a sudden flash of non-verbal communion, I "knew" that the trees didn't know or care about that human category information either – that it was actually irrelevant to their essential being, and it was irrelevant to the communion occurring between us.

Although some say that a unified consciousness involves an obliteration of differences between beings, I contend that empathy for the subjectivity of another being (whether tree or animal or human) includes the knowledge that we are distinctively different. Just as, in the state of being "in love," we may experience a telepathic and empathic oneness of thoughts and feelings while yet knowing, appreciating and cherishing the otherness of the beloved.

The interior mind-space of subjective consciousness is as infinitely vast as the outer space cosmos revealed by our astronomers. "No matter how far you travel in the realm of psyche, you will never come to the end of it," wrote Heraclitus. As an analogy, we may think of the space-time continuum as a transparent hollow sphere, where consciousness is the subjective, inner, concaveness and the objective, outer, convexity is matter and energy, in their ceaseless transformations.

We use the powerful methods science has developed for analyzing the objective complexities and details of our world. For a more complete and integrated understanding, we add to them the inner, sensuous, feeling-based, aesthetic appreciation of the essential, subjective interconnectedness of the ever-transforming web of life.

* * *

4
Radical Empiricism

The American philosopher William James (1842 –1910) approached the psychology of consciousness in his characteristic multifarious manner. He may have been the first person to use the concept of "field" in talking about consciousness: human beings have "fields of consciousness," which are always complex – containing body sensations, sense impressions, memories, thoughts, feelings, desires and "determinations of the will," in fact "a teeming multiplicity of objects and relations." He made it clear that when he spoke of the mind consisting of a "stream of thought," he actually meant not just thoughts, but images, sensations, intuitions, feelings, etc. flowing in streams.

William James explored the paranormal and mystical dimensions of consciousness that lie outside the boundaries of the scientific worldview. He pursued a life-long interest in what he called "exceptional mental states," including those found in hypnotism, somnambulism, hysteria, multiple personality, spirit possession and the inspirations of genius. In discussing such unusual states, he wrote that "the subject's mind loses its quality of unity, and lapses into a polypsychism of fields that genuinely co-exist and yet are…dissociated functionally." He wrote that "the mind is a confederation of psychic entities," anticipating later views on multiplicity and dissociation.

James's interest in unusual states of consciousness led him to experiment with nitrous oxide, or "laughing gas" as it was then known, an experience that reinforced his understanding of "trans-rational" states of consciousness. He wrote that the conclusion he drew from these experiences was

> that our normal waking consciousness, rational consciousness as we call it, is but one special type of consciousness, while all about it, parted from it by the filmiest of screens, there lie potential forms of consciousness entirely different. (James, 1901/1958, p. 228).

James wrote the above statement in his *The Varieties of Religious Experience*, probably his most influential book. In it he explored with great discernment the nature and significance of mystical or "conversion" experiences, by which he meant not only a person's change from one religion to another, but the process of attaining a sense of unity and the sacred dimension of life. In my book *The Unfolding Self* I adopted James' empirical, comparative approach to the study of transformative experiences, whether they are induced by spiritual practices, psychedelic substances or other means.

In addition to multiplicity, James was greatly impressed by the selectivity of consciousness. "The mind is at every stage a theatre of simultaneous possibilities. Consciousness consists in the comparison of these with each other, the selection of some, and the suppression of the rest." The self was the unifying principle in the multiple fields of consciousness, *and* the selective agency that expressed itself through its interests and the directing of attention. James' dictum – "my experience is what I agree to attend to" – anticipates my formula, discussed above:

Intention/interest → attention → awareness.

The Epistemology of Radical Empiricism

I have come to see that William James' writings on radical empiricism provide the epistemology of choice for the study of states of consciousness – ordinary or altered. Within the materialistic paradigm still presently ruling in scientific circles, any insights or learning gained from dreams, drug experiences, trances, intuitions, mystical ecstasies or the like, are seen as "merely subjective," and limited to those states, i. e. not having general applicability or "objective reality." The psychologist Charles Tart in an essay on "state-specific sciences" attempted to break the conceptual stranglehold of this paradigm by suggesting that observations made in a given state of consciousness could only be verified or replicated in that same state. This solution seems theoretically valid, but attended with practical difficulties.

William James started with the basic assumption of the empirical approach: all knowledge is derived from experience. Or, as the German proverb has it – *Die Erfahrung ist die Mutter der Wissenschaften* – "experience is the mother of the sciences." Radical empiricism applies this principle inclusively, not exclusively.

> I give the name of 'radical empiricism' to my *Weltanschauung*...To be radical an empiricism must neither admit into its construction any element that is not directly experienced, nor exclude from them any element that is directly experienced. (James, 1912/1996, p. 42)

This view provides a philosophical foundation for a scientific psychology of consciousness. All knowledge must be based on observation, i. e. experience; so far this view coincides with the empiricism of the natural and social sciences. It's the second statement that is truly 'radical' and that explains why James included religious and paranormal experiences in his investigations. The experiences in modified states of consciousness are currently excluded from materialistic, reductionistic science, as are all kinds of anomalous experiences, such as shamanic journeys, near-death experiences, and mystical or paranormal experiences. In a radical empiricism, they need not and should not be excluded.

After all, it is not where or how observations are made, that makes a field of study "scientific," it is what is done with the observations afterwards. Repeated systematic observations from the same observer, and replicating observations from others, is what distinguishes the scientific method from casual or haphazard observations, or those made with intentions other than gathering knowledge. The epistemology of radical empiricism posits that *it is possible to be objective about subjective experience*, using the accepted canons of the scientific method. The methodology of systematic introspection and phenomenology are the beginnings of such a more inclusive approach.

In Eastern systems of yoga and meditation, it has long been understood that reliable and replicable, i. e. objective, observations can be made in the interior landscapes of our experience. Such observations are in principle no different than the observations a biologist makes when looking through a microscope, or an astronomer with a telescope. The practice of "mindfulness" is an attitude in which self-reflexive consciousness is added to the primary data of subjective experience.

The Dalai Lama, in his discussions with Western scientists and philosophers, has said:

> if the scientific study of consciousness is ever to grow to full maturity – given that subjectivity is a primary element of consciousness – it will have to incorporate a fully developed and rigorous methodology of first-person empiricism. *(The Universe in a Single Atom, p. 160).*

With "first-person empiricism," we can supplement the observations made by others (e. g. measurements of brain waves) with observations by the subjects in their different inner states.

Of course, any and all observations, made in outer or inner realms, are subject to distortion and illusion, and therefore should always be submitted to replication, testing and verification by others in similar conditions. But without empirical observations we do not arrive at knowledge, although we may generate theories, beliefs, speculations and abstractions; as well as imaginative fantasies, which can in turn become the basis of story-telling and other art forms.

One of the most exciting consequences of adopting an epistemology of radical empiricism, in which no sources of new perceptions and observations will be ignored because of their provenance, is the opening up of vast new fields and possibilities of understanding, and a renewed bringing together of spiritual and scientific understandings into an inclusively integrated systems worldview.

* * *

5
States, Stages and Levels of Consciousness

We can, and should, distinguish three different paradigms for the scientific and philosophical study of consciousness. One is the notion of *states of consciousness* – both the ordinary states of waking, sleeping and dreaming, and non-ordinary or altered states, whether induced by drugs or other catalysts, and whether positive or negative. This is the paradigm that is the main focus of this book. This is also the paradigm which is most amenable to the testing of correlations between brain functions and consciousness.

Another, quite different paradigm, is the notion of *stages of consciousness development* – that in the course of the normal life-cycle human beings go through different phases; and that there are identifiable stages on the path of spiritual growth toward enlightenment. A third paradigm is that there are *levels, planes or dimensions of consciousness* – permanent structural features of the individual psyche and of our collective, shared external reality. We shall discuss the *stages* and *levels* paradigm in this chapter before going further in our investigation of states of consciousness in subsequent chapters.

Stages of Development in the Life-cycle

Western psychology has concerned itself with the stages of psychological development that a child goes through on its way to adulthood, such as Freud's psychosexual stages, or Jean Piaget's stages of cognitive development, or Lawrence Kohlberg's stages of moral development. The psychoanalyst Erik Erikson spoke of six stages of the life cycle with characteristic challenges in each stage. In the psychology of C. G. Jung we find the idea of two halves of the life-cycle, divided by the mid-life crisis: the first half of individualization – becoming a distinctive individual, and the second half of individuation, moving toward un-divided wholeness.

In my book and workshops on *Alchemical Divination*, I have identified three main stages of the life cycle: the *formative years* of childhood and young adulthood till the late 20s; the *productive or middle years* of the 30s, 40s and 50s; and the *elderhood years* of the 60s and beyond. In the formative phase, the main focus is on growing, developing and learning. Our sense of identity expands from being totally embedded in the family matrix, to becoming part of the larger community, society and world. The middle phase of adulthood is the time we settle down to a career, growing a family, pursuing our life's chosen goals and making a contribution to the community. The elder phase tends to be a time of reflection, of teaching and guiding the young, consideration of one's legacy and contemplation of what lies beyond death.

The stages paradigm comes at an understanding of consciousness in a quite different way than the concept of states, ordinary or non-ordinary. It is clear that these three different basic orientations towards life don't really amount to a permanently different state of consciousness. Rather, individuals in all three phases of their life cycle go through the ordinary states of waking, sleeping and dreaming; and they may experience involuntary or intentional altered states, ecstatic or traumatic, induced by external catalysts or occurring spontaneously.

The three-stage model is expanded to a four-stage one if we add the *prenatal epoch*. It is now widely accepted in the field of pre- and peri-natal psychology that the embryo and fetus is a fully sentient human being, exquisitely attuned to its parents and its environment. From my experience, I have come to understand that the prenatal stage of development is where the most deep-seated defensive identity patterns are established, often with long-lasting consequences for the individual.

Stages of Spiritual Growth

The second variant of the consciousness stages paradigm is found in the literature of Eastern and Western religious psychology, as well as in the literature of esoteric and transpersonal psychology. For example, in her book on Christian mysticism, Evelyn Underhill identified five stages on the mystic path: (1) awakening or conversion to divine reality; (2) purgation or purification; (3) illumination and ecstatic visions; (4) death of the old self, also called "dark night of the soul;" (5) union with the divine.

Another beautiful example, from the literature of Zen Buddhism, are the ten *Ox-Herding* pictures, symbolizing ten stages of progress toward enlightenment. In these allegorical images, the man represents the personal ego-self, and the wild ox that he first tracks and finds and then captures and tames, is his Buddha-nature, which is also his wild-animal nature. The first stage is called "searching for the ox," and the tenth, "entering the city with bliss-bestowing hands." This last image symbolically portrays the stage of the *bodhisattva* – in the Buddhist *mahayana* tradition, an enlightened being who returns from the *nirvana* state (where "both ox and man are transcended") to function in the world with compassion for the enlightenment of others.

One of the most complex and detailed maps of stages of consciousness evolution, both for the individual and for the collective culture, is found in the work of Ken Wilber. His model blends Western psychological theories about the development of consciousness from childhood to adult maturity with Eastern and esoteric teachings about stages of spiritual development.

It is important to recognize that such scenarios of spiritual development represent a different perspective than the altered states paradigm. Those who imagine that a yogic adept or Zen master is always in a state of enlightenment bliss or *nirvana* are confusing states and stages. The Buddhist texts are clear, for example, that Gautama Buddha entered into the state of *nirvana* (where there is not the arising of even a single thought or impulse) and stayed there for eight days; and then "came down," as it were, and worked the rest of his life to teach and preach, found monasteries, walk, eat and drink among others, until the death of his physical form.

We can understand the difference between these paradigms in terms of the difference between "oneness" and "wholeness." Oneness, called *samadhi* in the yoga traditions and *nirvana* in Buddhist teachings, refers to a state of consciousness where there is no perception of distinctions, just undifferentiated blissful, awareness, without any content. Wholeness on the other hand refers to the integrated, yet open-ended and evolving totality of our being. As we move toward wholeness (in a process that C. G.

Jung called *individuation*), there may be experiences of states of mystical oneness, as well as states of being lost and distracted by illusions, and experiences of functioning in our chosen life-paths and communities.

My last example of the stages paradigm is from the writings of the 19th century German scientist-mystic **Gustav Theodore** Fechner. Here we encounter a three-stage model of human existence, remarkably perceptive in its understanding of human development and the mysteries of the soul, and yet that is expressed in purely philosophical language, without the trappings of any religious doctrine, either Western or Eastern. In Fechner's view, the three phases of every human existence are: (1) the prenatal phase, in which we grow the somatic equipment for our embodied life, from the seed-form of conception to birth; (2) the middle phase between birth and death, in which we grow and nourish the divine soul-seed through our life experiences; and (3) the post-mortem phase of the hereafter, where we are liberated from the limitations of the embodied stage.

The Paradigm of Levels or Dimensions of Consciousness

Conceptual maps of different realms of consciousness and reality are found in the Asian spiritual traditions, in indigenous shamanistic worldviews, in Western esoteric and mystical writings, and in 20th century psychological theories. It is far beyond the scope of this book to attempt anything like a systematic comparison of these different mappings. I will only briefly describe selected examples of such dimensional theories and teachings, in order to clarify the nature of this paradigm and how it differs from the paradigms of states and stages.

It should be understood that the levels of consciousness are not temporary states of consciousness – rather they are permanent structural features of our own being, and of the world around us. One could say that during particular states of consciousness, such as a dream state or a meditation, we are focused "in" a particular realm or level. In what I am calling the *functional waking state*, we are focused in the *time-space material level*. In the Sufi tradition we hear the metaphor that the human being inhabits a many-storied mansion, but has long lived exclusively on the ground floor – pointing to the possibility of expanding or raising consciousness into the "higher" realms, during meditative or visionary states. We may suppose that the higher our spiritual development, the more we have conscious and intentional access to all the many realms.

Shamanism. Shamanistic cosmologies worldwide usually distinguish between Upper, Middle and Lower worlds, although in some traditions, like the Nordic-Germanic, there are nine worlds that the shaman may visit and explore in the course of his/her healing journeys. Experientially, Upper World journeys are out-of-body states in which one moves upward, perhaps accompanied by a bird ally; while on Lower World journeys one moves downward into a cave or opening in the ground, and emerges after a while into a distinctively different open landscape. According to Michael Harner's integrative explication of cross-cultural shamanic teachings, the Upper and Lower worlds are mostly inhabited by spirits that are compassionate towards us humans and inclined to help or guide us in our quests for healing and guidance. By contrast, the Middle world, in both its material and non-material aspects, is the trickiest to explore, because of the multiple possibilities of illusions, attachments and distractions.

Western religion and psychology. In the teachings of Catholicism, long the dominant ideology in the West, there was traditionally a four-level model of the psyche: Body-Mind-Soul-Spirit. Somewhere along in the Middle Ages, perhaps due to the influence of the Trinitarian doctrine of the Church, this model devolved to a three-fold model of Body, Mind and Spirit. By the time of Descartes, the three-fold model had shrunk to the twofold of body and mind, or matter and mind – *res extensa* and *res cogitans*. The journey of the incredible diminishing psyche reached its climax in the psychology of the early 20th century, by which time all notions of divinity or spirit had been expunged from the natural and social sciences. In the Behaviorism of J. B. Watson and B. F. Skinner only bodily behavior is amenable to scientific investigation. The mind does not exist – for the behaviorist, it is an unknowable "black box."

Western esoteric teachings. In Western esoteric traditions, which I studied intensively in my ten years in the School of Actualism, a seven-layer model of the human constitution is described – ranging from the densest and heaviest (the physical body), through the intermediate or personality bodies of lesser density, on up to the highest level of oneness with the Divine Mother-Father Creator. In these teachings, the difference between levels is formulated in terms of an acoustic analogy: *the dimensions differ in vibratory frequency rate,* like the notes of an octave, with the physical body being the lowest frequency, densest form, and the only one visible to ordinary perception. Just like the notes of different frequency in a chord, these subtle bodies and dimensions can co-exist and coincide with the time-space world, without interference. In the iconography of Indian and Buddhist art, the multi-bodied nature and capabilities of advanced spirit beings are portrayed symbolically as deities with many pairs of arms and heads.

Freudian psychology. The influence of Sigmund Freud on 20th century Western thought has been profound, and his views have, to a large extent, become the mainstream psychology of Western culture. Freud had several models of psychic structure: one was called "psychodynamic" – a kind of hydraulic image with drives, impulses and defenses. There was also a model called "topographical" – which consisted of layers arranged somehow one on top of the other. The bottom layer is the *unconscious* (what we're totally not conscious of); the next layer is *pre-conscious* (what we could become conscious of, if we chose to); and at the top, like the above-water tip of the iceberg, is the *conscious* – our everyday conscious ego-mind.

It is important to recognize the implicit spatial metaphors in this psychic model. Unconscious mental images are not really located "below" conscious ones. Actually, they're not really located anywhere. Quantum physicists now tell us that awareness is non-local, like photons and sub-atomic particles. Furthermore, the implicit spatial metaphor is compounded by linguistic reification ("thing-making"). When we name an abstraction, we concretize it and make it somehow more real. In actuality, we know that there is neither an entity nor a place called "the Unconscious." There are, of course, feelings, thoughts and impulses of which we are not aware – until we become aware of them.

Jungian and transpersonal psychology. C. G. Jung, as is well known, broadened the conception of the unconscious mind, saying it included not only the libidinal and aggressive impulses that Freud had emphasized, but also creative insights and intuitions. Whereas Freud's natural world metaphor for the unconscious was to compare it to the sea, with its unknown depths and terrors, Jung suggested the metaphor that the unconscious was like the night-sky, shrouded in darkness, but seeded with sparks of light, symbolic of insights and intuitions.

Jung also posited a *collective unconscious*, a realm of *archetypes* – primordial images and thought-forms shared more or less by all human beings. In our dreams and visions our personal imagery may be blended with the archetypes of the collective unconscious. For example, an individual's feelings and perceptions of their personal mother may be bound up with the Great Mother Goddess archetype. Later Jungian analysts and scholars drew a further distinction: inserting a layer they called *cultural unconscious*, between the personal and the collective. For example, the image of the Madonna or Virgin Mary is the archetypal Great Mother expressed in the cultural symbolism of the Christian West.

We can see that Eastern and Western esoteric traditions have presented integrated worldviews in which the physical, psychic and spiritual aspects of our being are recognized and named. Western psychological schools, whether the cognitive, behavioral, social science or psychoanalytic strands, are the inheritors of the Western materialist, mechanistic worldview in which the spiritual dimensions are considered the domain of religion and disconnected from science. The writings of Jung and his followers in the depth psychology traditions, basing their theories on clinical observations made in the course of psychotherapy and dream analysis, accommodate the spiritual dimensions of human experience as being primordial images or archetypes contained in the collective unconscious.

Living systems worldview. From the perspective of an ecological systems view, as I have suggested in my book *Green*

Psychology, the Jungian "collective unconscious" (with both its conscious and unconscious elements) is actually the species-wide human level of consciousness – shared by and accessible by all of humanity, in varying degrees. But once we recognize that human consciousness is not the only kind, we can see that there are levels of consciousness "below" or "beyond" the human species level: the consciousness of all animals, of all organic life, the Gaian or biospheric consciousness of planet Earth, the universal or cosmic consciousness of the mystics.

I believe, along with scientists such as Fritjof Capra, Joanna Macy, Ervin Laszlo, David Korten and others, that a living systems worldview will be and should be considered the foundational science of the present age. In such a worldview, reality, both microcosmic and macrocosmic, is recognized to be organized in many levels or dimensions, and the various sciences study the patterned inter-relationships between and within levels. Such a multi-dimensional perspective is most amenable to the inclusion of the observations made in different states of consciousness and the mappings of the different realms of consciousness into a truly integrative and holistic worldview.

* * *

6
The Set and Setting Model

A state of consciousness may be defined as the subjective space or field within which the different contents of consciousness, such as thoughts, feelings, images, perceptions, sensations, intuitions, memories and so forth, function in patterned inter-relationships. Furthermore, a state of consciousness always implies a definite division of the stream of time, between two transition points. For example, we are in the sleep state between the time of *falling asleep* and the time of *waking up*. We are in the functional waking state, also called "ordinary state," between the moments of waking up and of falling asleep. States of drug or alcohol intoxication extend from the time of ingestion to the time of "sobering up" or "coming down." A meditative state or a hypnotic trance state begins and ends with transitions we refer to as "going in" or "coming back," as if crossing some kind of threshold.

Although we can (sometimes) anchor the subjective state transitions to external objective (clock) time, it is important to recognize that each state has its own subjective time-line or time-stream. For example, in dreams both time and space are quite different than in the waking state. In a dream we may meet with a beloved person who lives thousands of miles away – and it takes no "real time" to travel to this meeting. Distance in the dream state is not geographical but emotional, a function of affinity and interest. Indeed, in dreams and other deep states we may find ourselves meeting and conversing with someone who is dead – having transcended altogether the space-time boundaries of ordinary reality. *At the transitions between states, there is a discontinuity and we switch into a different time-stream and a different mind-space.*

As I pointed out in chapter 1, the notion of an altered state has acquired a certain connotation of abnormality, perhaps due to its association with drug states, even though we are all familiar with the profoundly different states of dreaming and sleeping. For this reason, I have come to think that it is important for us to learn to recognize and identify the times and situations when we are functioning in a markedly different than usual mode, i. e. in a different state.

If we can identify the transition or trigger points when the mode of consciousness changes, we can learn to utilize the positive states according to our conscious intention: for example, a musician or other artist might find that a period of meditation facilitates accessing the flow state that heightens creative expression. Perhaps even more important for our wellbeing, we must learn to navigate out of negative, destructive states: for example, learning to recognize the verbal triggers for an altered state of rage is an important aspect of anger management in interpersonal relations.

The transitions between different states are intersection points of different time-lines, where we can consciously choose to move along another time-line into a more expansive space, pregnant with new possibilities. If we don't choose consciously, then we will be shunted into another state according to the prevailing winds of karma, or our habitual reactions.

Some altered states are generally considered positive, healthy and expansive, associated with deeper understanding and spiritual value: we may think of mystical oneness, ecstasy, transcendence, vision, hypnotherapeutic trance, creative inspiration, erotic union, shamanic journey, cosmic consciousness, *samadhi, nirvana, satori*. Other altered states are considered negative, unhealthy, contractive, associated with delusion, psychopathology, destruction and conflict: we can recognize the altered states of depression, anxiety, trauma, psychosis, madness, hysteria, rage, mania, addictions (alcohol, narcotics, stimulants) and behavioral compulsions and obsessions (sexuality, violence, gambling, spending).

The diagram (p. 44) shows what I am calling a heuristic general model of states of consciousness. It is heuristic rather than explanatory, in that it offers a framework for thinking about states, rather than a causal theory. The model can also facilitate research on the neural or biochemical changes correlated with different states.

It is useful think of a kind of spectrum of the scope of change. We may change our thinking, our beliefs, opinions and attitudes, for example, in reading a book or listening to a lecture, without registering a change of state. Our emotional state or mood may also vary, from happy to sad, "down" to "up," while still within our normal functional state of consciousness. Even intensely new and different sensations, such as the unexpected taste pleasure of a gourmet meal, or the unexpected distasteful smell of a polluted environment, need not trigger an altered state.

However, when changes in our subjective body image occur together with changes in the perception of time and space, then

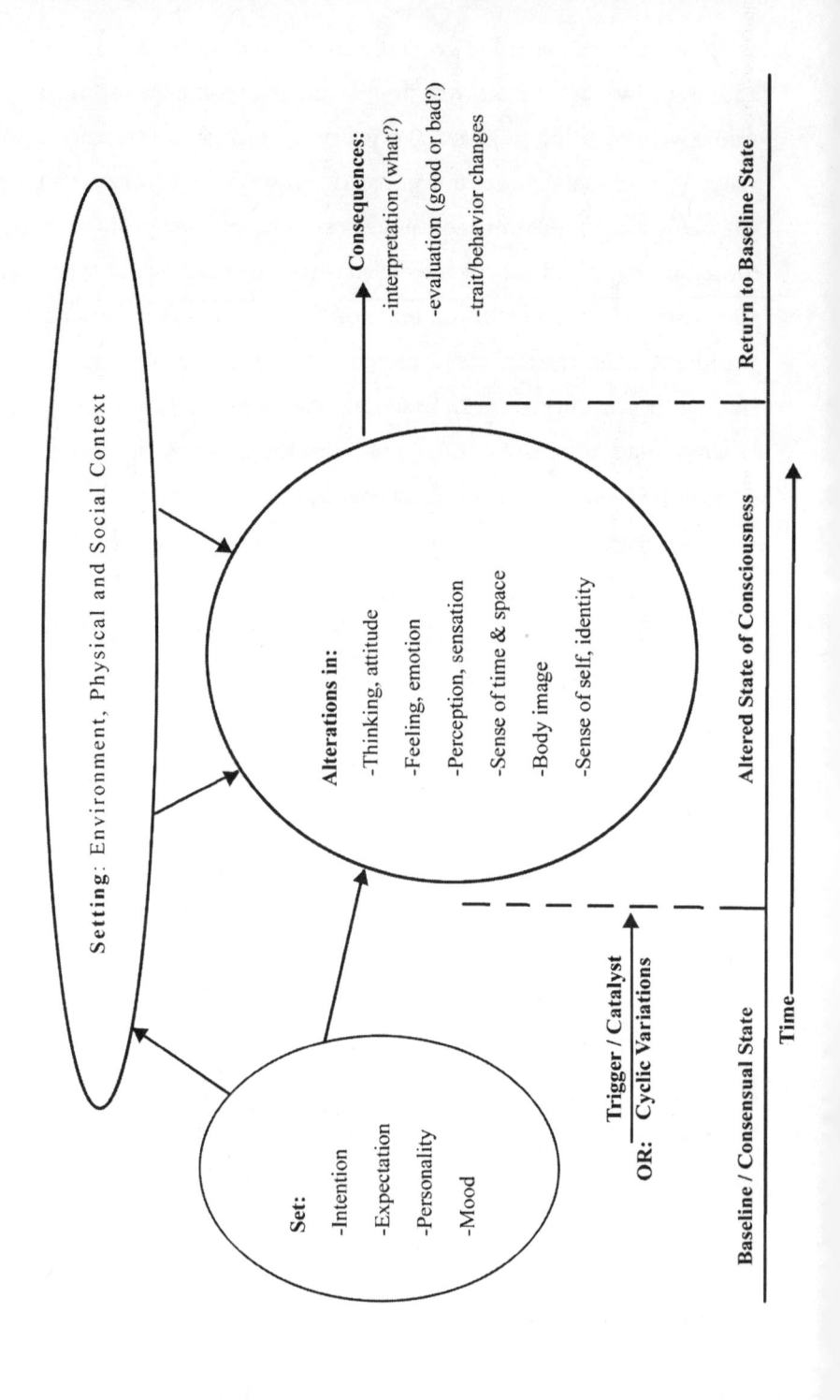

Setting: Environment, Physical and Social Context

Set:
- Intention
- Expectation
- Personality
- Mood

Trigger / Catalyst
OR: Cyclic Variations

Alterations in:
- Thinking, attitude
- Feeling, emotion
- Perception, sensation
- Sense of time & space
- Body image
- Sense of self, identity

Consequences:
- interpretation (what?)
- evaluation (good or bad?)
- trait/behavior changes

Baseline / Consensual State | Altered State of Consciousness | Return to Baseline State

Time

we definitely recognize a different state. Then, "we're not in Kansas anymore," as Dorothy said, when her experiential world was turned topsy-turvy by the hurricane. In emergency medicine, questions about our orientation in time and place *(What day is this? What place is this?)* are used to diagnose the state of consciousness of someone possibly in shock or trauma. The most profoundly altered states are those in which the sense of identity or self-image are abolished: these include the states of ego-death or depersonalization that may occur in psychosis, as well as states of *nirvana* or oneness that may occur in mysticism.

The key to understanding the content of a psychedelic experience, as formulated by Timothy Leary, Frank Barron and colleagues (including myself) in the early days of the Harvard Psilocybin Research Project, was the "set-and-setting" hypothesis. This hypothesis, which has been widely accepted within the field, states that the content of a psychedelic experience is not so much a function of pharmacology, i. e. a "drug effect," but rather a function of the set, which is all the internal factors of expectation, intention, mood, temperament, attitude; and the setting, which is the external environment, both physical and social, and including the attitudes and intentions of whoever provides, initiates or **accompanies the experience.** The drug is regarded as a trigger, or catalyst, propelling the individual into a different state of consciousness or mind-space, in which the vividness and contextual qualities of sense perceptions are greatly magnified.

This hypothesis helped the Harvard researchers to understand how the same drugs could be seen and used as inducing a model psychosis (*psychotomimetic*), as an adjunct to psychoanalysis (*psycholytic*), a treatment for addiction or stimulus to creativity (*psychedelic*), a facilitator of shamanic healing journeys (*entheogenic*);

or even, as used by the US Army and CIA, as a truth-serum type of tool for obtaining secrets from enemy spies. Of the two factors of set and setting, set or intention is clearly primary, since the set ordinarily determines what kind of setting one will choose for the experience.

According to the heuristic model I am proposing, we extend the set and setting hypothesis to all alterations of consciousness, no matter by what trigger they are induced, and even those states that recur cyclically and regularly, such as sleeping and waking. In those cyclic alterations of consciousness, we recognize that internal biochemical events normally trigger the transition to sleeping or waking consciousness, but external factors may also provide a catalyst. For example, lying in bed, in darkness, triggers changes in melatonin levels in the pineal gland, which in turn promote the transition to sleep. Other biochemical changes in the brain, brighter light and the sounds of an alarm, can be the trigger for awakening, again meditated by cyclical biochemical changes. In addition, external factors such as sedative or stimulant drugs, loud noises or peaceful music, stress or relaxation, can also trigger variations in the sleep-wakefulness cycle.

Clearly, the content of our dreams can be analyzed as a function of set, our internal preoccupations during the day, as well as the environment in which we find ourselves. Practitioners of "dream incubation" make deliberate use of that principle, consciously formulating certain questions related to their inner process or problems, as they enter the world of night-time dreaming. In the temples of Asclepius in ancient Greece, those who suffered physical or psychic illnesses were guided to incubate diagnostic and healing dreams.

As I described in *Alchemical Divination*, being conscious of the specific intention, question or set preceding any trance-like therapeutic or shamanic state is the key to accessing healing and guidance from inner spiritual sources – regardless of whether the particular trance induction method is shamanic drumming, hypnosis or entheogenic plant medicines like ayahuasca.

After all, it is obvious that even our experiences in ordinary waking states, such as that of the reader perusing this text, and that of the author writing it, are determined by the internal factors of intention, set or interest, and the external setting where the reading, and the writing, are taking place.

In the framework of this set-and-setting model, after our mode of conscious functioning returns to the baseline state (which some also call *consensual reality* state), comes the time for evaluation and interpretation. Keeping in mind the two transition points, into and out of the altered state, makes it easier to separate the experience itself from our thoughts and judgments about it. Making this separation is the essence of the phenomenological method, pioneered by Edmund Husserl and Maurice Merleau-Ponty in philosophy, and by Bert Hellinger in family constellation therapy. It is also the core of mindfulness (*vipassana*) meditation practice, where you just observe and note your thoughts, feelings and sensations, but do not analyze, track or evaluate them.

Evaluative judgment is usually the first and immediate reaction after any altered state – e. g. that was a bad trip or bad dream, or, this was a wonderful or inspiring experience. Researchers in neuroscience have discovered that evaluative feeling judgments on our experience originate in the mammalian limbic system (especially the amygdala) and may be an evolutionary residue of an instinctual survival reaction to perceived threat.

Evaluative judgments do not convey much information about an experience however. How much do you really learn about a film, for example, when your friend merely tells you that she liked it, or that it was terrible?

A crucial aspect of what follows an altered state experience is the application and integration, or lack thereof, into one's ongoing life. We need to go beyond first judgments and associative interpretations, and ask ourselves — what does this experience mean to me or what do I learn from it? Does a mystic vision of oneness with the divine lead to a morally better, happier and more saintly life? Do the insights from a healing vision or dream lead to a problem resolution? Does the depressed state I'm experiencing mean I have a depressive personality, or is it a temporary reaction to a stressful situation?

* * *

An Exercise in Altered State Recognition

This is a self-reflective exercise I have often used in my classes on altered states of consciousness. Pick one positive and one negative altered state experience from your recent experience, perhaps within the last year. (I suggest you don't pick two different drug experiences, but have at least one of the two involve a non-drug catalyst). Then, for each experience, having identified the trigger, ask yourself what was your set – the inner mood, expectation or intention, and what was the setting – the physical and social context of the experience?

You will probably find that recognizing the intention and context of the altered state, can give you significant insight into the phenomenology of the experience, as well as your subsequent interpretation of it. Even those familiar with psychedelic drugs, where set/setting factors are particularly known to be important, often tend to attribute differences in their experiences to the different chemistry, rather than look to the intentions and contexts.

7
Waking, Sleeping, Dreaming, Meditating

When I was a child I used to try to catch the exact moment when I would slip from waking to sleep – only to wake up hours later, disappointed that I had somehow missed it. Later, I found out that paying close attention to that transition phase is one of the practices of the Tibetan Buddhist yoga of dreams. What we call the ordinary or waking state (the "baseline state" in terms of the heuristic model) may also be called, as my friend Charles Tart has pointed out, the "consensual" state, because we orient ourselves and navigate our way through space and time, using the consensual reality models of our culture. We may think of the waking state as the *functional state*, when we are most attuned to the time-and-space dimension of reality.

The functional waking state involves a period of time demarcated by two transitions – *waking up* and *falling asleep* – alternating with the sleep state for the two phases of the diurnal cycle. Like all forms of life, whether animal, plant, fungal or cellular, our human organism is embedded in a *circadian rhythm* (approximately 24 hours) as the part of the Earth we inhabit turns towards or away from the Sun. Melatonin, the sleep hormone, is secreted from the pineal gland as the daylight dims and the vegetative nervous system moves into parasympathetic restorative mode. As the dawn returns, melatonin levels decline and adrenaline and various corticosteroids fuel sympathetic activation for daytime activity, effort and movement. Of course, these basic alternating cycles of sleep and wakefulness can be, and often are, modified intentionally by the demands of work, and may be disrupted by stress. But even people isolated in lightless caves for long periods, still tend to sleep for roughly equivalent amounts of time.

The phase transitions, "falling asleep" and "waking up" are described consistently in different languages, using implicit spatial metaphors that capture something of the experience of those transitions. Why is it we don't ever say, or subjectively feel, that we "wake down" or "rise asleep?" In German, *aufwachen* ("open-waking") and *einschlafen* ("in-sleeping") suggest a flower-like opening and closing. In French, *s'endormir* also points to the reflexive, inward movement into sleep; and *se reveiller* ("to reveal oneself") the opening, expansive movement into wakefulness. When I open my eyes and wake up, awareness expands, relative to the dream/sleep world I was in before: here is my body, in my bed with my partner, in my room in the house where I live, and outside the window is the garden, the street, the larger world. The private, inner world of sleep and the idiosyncratic reality of dream-time recede, as our senses open, ready for functioning in the time-space reality.

The transition from sleep to wakefulness is one of the exemplary metaphors for the heightened or expanded spiritual awareness of Zen masters, yogis and mystics. This metaphor implies an important philosophical worldview: the view that our perception of reality, our ordinary awareness of the world, is a kind of dream, illusory and transient. In Buddhism, as well as in Vedanta and

Yoga psychology, what we think of as the ordinary waking state consciousness is called *avidya,* a "not-knowing" or *unconsciousness.* The not-knowing is not the ignorance of this or that information, but rather an unconsciousness of our true spiritual essence. When we awaken in this spiritual sense, we become more aware of the actual larger world around us, as well as more in tune with the essential spiritual core of our being. As the *Katha Upanishad* states: "That being who is awake in those that sleep … that is *Brahman,* that is called the Immortal."

The phase transition from the waking into the sleep state has much in common with the transition we call dying – including the prone and passive posture of the body. In Greek mythology, *Hypnos* (god of sleep) and *Thanatos* (god of death) were twin brothers, their dark robes and wings symbolizing the closing of outer perception and the release from body awareness, common to both transitions.

The ultradian cycle in sleep and wakefulness

Modern sleep researchers have identified four stages of sleep, with characteristically different EEG wave patterns. It takes progressively longer to awaken someone from the deeper stages, with lower-frequency, **higher-amplitude EEG.** The sleeping brain descends through the stages in about 30 to 40 minutes, then re-ascends through stages 3 and 2 and enters a 10 minute period of REM (rapid eye movement) dreaming sleep – almost to **wakefulness.** The entire sleep-dream cycle, called *ultradian,* takes about 90 minutes ($\pm$ 20), and is repeated four or five times during the night.

✎ = partial awakening with body movements

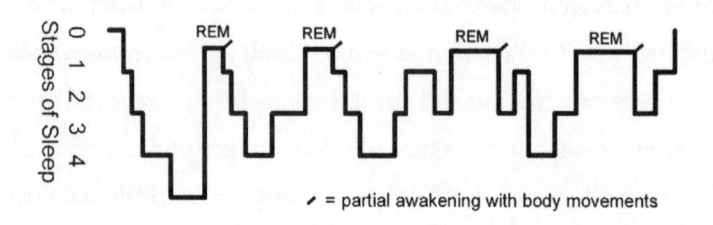

10pm 11pm 12am 1am 2am 3am 4am 5am 6am 7am

The REM stage of dreaming sleep has higher-frequency EEG waves similar to the waking state, but the lower muscle activity (EMG) of non-dreaming sleep. This correlation supports the idea that during REM dreaming sleep the brain is sorting through and processing perceptions and thoughts, while the body musculature is safely passive. It was the discovery, in the 1950s, that measurable eye-movements (REM) were correlated with the dreaming phase of sleep, as well as distinctive brain-wave patterns (EEG), that led Western science to first establish that these were two distinctly different states of consciousness.

In the ancient Indian Vedanta and Yoga teachings the distinctiveness of dream-sleep and deep sleep was already recognized, on the basis of systematic introspections. According to these teachings in the dreaming phase *(svapna)* the mind is occupied with interior thoughts and images, and in deep sleep *(sushupti)* we are totally absorbed in the transpersonal, spiritual realms, and rarely remember anything. A fourth state of consciousness, *turiya*, is recognized in Indian yoga – and said to be a state of meditative oneness, akin to *samadhi*.

From the perspective of Western psychology, these four basic common states can be understood in terms of different configurations of attention. In the waking state, we focus perception on the sense objects of the external world, and the inner world sensorium is background (though strong internal sensations, vivid feelings or persistent thoughts may capture our attention). In the relaxed, meditative state, when the eyes are typically closed, this figure-ground relation is reversed: the inner world sensorium (e. g. the flow of breath, the stream of thoughts and feelings) becomes the foreground of attention and external sense objects become background (again, unless disrupted by a strong stimulus such as a loud noise). In the dream state, with the outer world more or less completely closed out, the figural focus is on visual imagery and emotions, and other aspects of the inner sensorium are background. In the non-dream sleep state, the selectivity of focus is suspended and everything is reduced to (back) ground.

The 90-minute ultradian cycle, associated with dream (REM) and non-dream sleep (NREM), has also been observed to occur during the daytime waking state. When people were asked to write down their thoughts and images every 10 minutes – it was found that roughly every 90 minutes ideation became more fantastic, less reality-focused, more diffuse and dreamlike. People in meetings start to look out the window, or day-dream about their vacations or their lovers. There is evidence that during the dream-trance part of the cycle, the right cerebral hemisphere, the one concerned with imagery more than language, is more activated.

Some have suggested that we could take advantage of this ultradian physiological cycle to schedule 10-15 minute rest and relaxation breaks to coincide with the down-time of this cycle – and avoid decision-making during such times. The great American hypnotherapist-healer Milton Erickson had developed his powers of observation to such an extent that he would notice the minute physiological indications of what he called a "naturalistic trance" (the flushing forehead, the throbbing pulse in the throat, the pearls of sweat on the upper lip) and then just encourage the patient's movement into hypnotic trance.

There is an interesting parallel to these research findings on the ultradian cycle, in the tantra yoga teaching of two energy channels (*nadis*) and the innate cycle of alternate nostril breathing. There are said to be two subtle energy channels, *ida* and *pingala,* coiling like two snakes around the central channel *(sushumna),* which is aligned with but not identical to the spinal column. The left channel, *ida nadi,* carries cooling, relaxing, moist and lunar energy; we activate it by breathing through the left nostril, which energizes the whole left side of the body and therefore also the right brain hemisphere. The right channel, *pingala ida,* carries warming, stretching, dry and solar energy; we activate it (and the left brain hemisphere) by focusing breath through the right nostril.

In tantra yoga practice, you try to consciously balance the energy-flow through the two side channels and the central vertical axis, for improvement in health and well-being. Unconsciously, in turning from one side to the other while sleeping, the breath and the energy flows more on the side that is uppermost – thus balancing the ultradian cycle of alternate nostril breathing.

Brain wave variations in the waking state

With the discovery and application of EEG biofeedback technology, four different phases within the waking state have been identified as well, correlated with distinct brain-wave frequency patterns. A calm, eyes-closed, meditative state is associated with brain-waves in the 8-13 cps (cycles-per-second) range, called *alpha*; when people are given auditory feed-back of the presence of alpha waves, they can readily learn to put themselves into a calm, meditative state. And the deeper the concentrative absorption, the more coherent the alpha frequencies recorded from different areas of the brain. When people are functioning in the regular, eyes-open, thinking and imaging mode, irregular, mixed frequencies in the *beta* range, above 13 cps are recorded. With experienced meditators doing complex visualizations, and insight meditations, coherent brain-waves in the high beta range (40+ cps, also called *gamma* waves) can also be observed. With meditation practice, as well as with brainwave biofeedback training, individuals can learn to maintain their focus in one particular

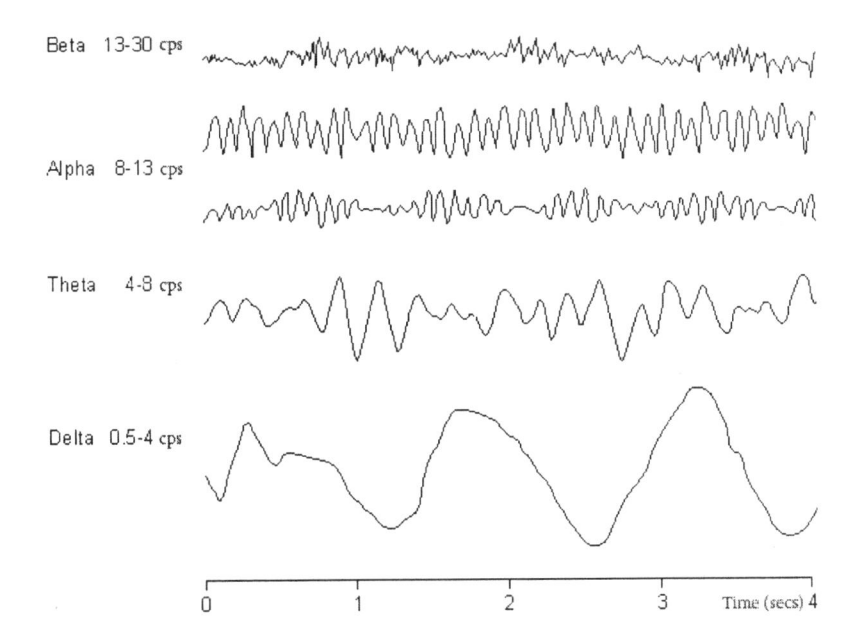

Beta 13-30 cps

Alpha 8-13 cps

Theta 4-8 cps

Delta 0.5-4 cps

0   1   2   3   Time (secs) 4

frequency-band and state for longer periods of time.

Brain-waves in the *theta* frequency range (4-8 cps) are associated with the semi-conscious transitional phase traditionally called *twilight sleep* or *waking dream,* where unusually rich imagery may drift through mental space, while the body is

55

virtually immobilized. Some artists and inventors obtain creative inspirations from this state, and healing imagery can occur as well, though it is hard to maintain as one tends to drift off into the *delta* range of the slower frequencies (0. 5-4 cps) of deeper sleep. Brain waves in the theta and delta range are recorded in stage 1 of the sleep cycle as we descend, and during REM sleep as we partially re-emerge from the dreamless sleep of stages 2, 3 and 4. In any particular individual recording of brain wave patterns, mixed frequencies may occur, along with bursts of coherence, which suggests that the different states of consciousness merge and drift into one another other under normal conditions.

What do dreams mean?

Neuroscientists studying the brains of humans and other mammals have emphasized the physiological restorative and biochemical rebalancing functions of sleep. Consolidation of daytime learning and re-processing of perceptual memories may also be occurring while the sensory-motor systems are quiescent. Indeed, enhanced learning and cognitive problem solving after sleep has been demonstrated in laboratory studies. Dreams, from this reductionist perspective, are viewed as the incoherent residual detritus of daytime reality-focus, a meaningless waste-stream of discarded thought-fragments.

On the other hand, depth psychologists have seen dreams, in Freud's words, as "the royal road to the unconscious." A vast literature on the interpretation of dream symbolism and on working with dreams in psychotherapy exists, with Freudians focusing on how dream imagery reflects our sexual and aggressive conflicts, and Jungians broadening the scope to recognize creative inspirations and spiritual visions coming into consciousness through dreams. For myself, the visions and insights I've received through dreams have been at least as meaningful, varied and innovative as those received from psychedelic drug states. For some visions I've had, I can't remember anymore whether they came to me in a dream, a psychedelic state, or a meditation. In all cases, I do not take the images or visions received at their face-value, but rather use further reflection and divination to discern their meaning and relevance.

Most Western dream theories, including even the Jungian, regard the imagery and visions received in dreams as being creations of the human unconscious, whether personal or collective archetypal. Here is the big dividing line between the Western scientific worldview and the worldview of indigenous, shamanistic societies: in the latter, dreams and the beings we encounter in them can be as real as the beings we encounter in the waking state of ordinary reality.

In some shamanistic societies, such as the Australian aboriginals, dream reality, or *dreamtime* as they call it, is considered more real, in fact the originating source of the reality we encounter in the waking state. For example, women and men may connect in dreamtime at conception with a child that intends to be born into their family. Dreams are, like shamanic drumming journeys, among the ways in which shamans might obtain diagnostic information about a patient. Among the Pomo Indians of Northern California, for example, a healer, such as the revered elder Essie Parrish, might listen to their client's request, and then tell them to come back the next day, or in a couple of days, giving the healer some nights for diagnostic dreams.

Probably because of my contact with shamanic practitioners as well as with yogic practices, my own worldview has evolved over time, so that when I've dreamed of meetings with friends, teachers or colleagues, I tend to hold these in my mind as real – either (a) as memories of meetings in the waking state; or (b) as anticipatory visions of meetings and conversations to come; or (c) as encounters with the soul or spirit of that individual. I've also practiced (and continue to practice) personal problem solving or divination through dream incubation: before going to sleep, I hold the question in my mind, and that set or intention then provides clues to the interpretation of the dream's symbolism. Many artists and scientists have reported obtaining inspiration for their art or insight for their research interests in dreams.

The occurrence of telepathy in dreams was demonstrated in an experimental setting in studies by Montague Ullman and Stanley Krippner in the 1960s. In these experiments, a person sitting in a room adjacent to where a subject was sleeping, would look at a picture and intentionally "send" the image to the sleeper. The matches between the dream imagery and the picture, evaluated independently, were statistically significant. Some time ago, my friend Stanley Krippner was giving a talk at Esalen about his dream telepathy research. I was scheduled to come and join the group at Esalen as well. On the night before I drove to Esalen from San Francisco, I dreamed of some horses galloping out of the sea. This was in fact the theme of one of the pictures from his research that Krippner had presented to the group at Esalen, as I found out later.

Friendship and close personal relationship between individuals facilitates the occurrence of telepathic and precognitive dreams. There are numerous anecdotal accounts of precognitive warning dreams: for example, a woman dreams the plane her husband is scheduled to take will crash, and thus is able to warn him.

Through my own repeated experiences, I've come to the view that many of our dreams are anticipatory visions or rehearsals of our probable futures, perhaps as often as they are the reprocessing of the events and memories of our past.

In dreams, as in other altered states, we are released from the strict confines of the time-space level of reality: we can visit and converse with a beloved person who lives thousands of miles away, and it takes no real time to travel there. Indeed, we can have meaningful dream encounters and conversations with persons who are "dead" in the physical world, but living in the inner dimensions or spirit world. Like closeness, distance in dreams is emotional distance, and can be bridged by affinity, by desire and longing.

In recent years, the phenomenon of lucidity, knowing that you are dreaming while in the dream, has attracted a great deal of attention. The psychologist Stephen LaBerge and others have developed training programs to enhance dream lucidity. LaBerge also invented a biofeedback device that gives the sleeper a signal that REM is occurring, thus facilitating awakening *in* the dream — but not *from* the dream. Lucid dreams are often associated with flying dreams – both are states where we can move intentionally in another dimension of reality.

As I pointed out in chapter 3, lucid dreaming relates to ordinary dreaming the way mindfulness relates to the ordinary waking state. Lucidity in dreams, like mindfulness in the waking state, affords more choice and more possibilities of movement. The most commonly experienced moments of dream lucidity occur when we realize that a painful or unpleasant experience we are having is a dream – and promptly exit from the nightmare.

Here is where lucid dreaming work converges with yogic dream practices. In Buddhism the term for a state of consciousness is *bardo* – which literally means "between phase," and we have seen that every state of consciousness is defined by its transition points in the time stream. Whereas in Vedanta and Yoga, four different common states are identified (as in Western psychology), in Buddhism sleeping and dreaming states are combined and, along with the meditation state, make up the three *bardos* that we cycle through all our lives between birth and death. (In addition to those three, there are the three *bardos*, or intermediate states, between death and rebirth, that are spoken of in the *Tibetan Book of the Dead*). There is a text by the great 5th century Indian philosopher Naropa, called the *The Yogas of the Six Bardos*, which describes the practices by means of which one can attain enlightenment or liberation from each of the six *bardo* states.

In this text by Naropa, there are verses epitomizing the yogic liberation practice for each of the six *bardos*. Here is my version of the yogic instructions for the three common *bardo* states.

Now that the bardo *of waking life has dawned upon me,*
Developing awareness without distraction,
I will listen, reflect and meditate,
As I pursue the path to enlightenment,
Through investigation of the nature of perception and mind.
Now that I have come into human form,
I will not waste this lifetime in idleness.

Now as I enter the bardo *of dreaming,*
I will abandon corpse-like unconscious sleeping,
Keeping awareness mindfully in its natural state.
Lucidly recognizing my dreams, I will practice the transformations.
Avoiding the unconsciousness of animal sleep,
I will practice merging the dreaming and waking consciousness.

Now as I enter the bardo *of deep meditation,*
I will try to let go all distractions and illusions,
And focus with complete concentration in the unitive state.
I will visualize clearly while moving smoothly through the stages.
Meditating one-pointedly and leaving aside all mundane concerns,
I will not succumb to craving or anger.

* * *

Suggested Practices for Working with Dreams and Sleep

1 - Monitor your sleep cycle and eliminate sleep debt.

Sleep deprivation is both a cause and a consequence of stress and many psychosomatic disorders. Conversely, sufficient sleep has been shown to strengthen the immune system, speed recovery from illness, improve learning and enhance creativity. Many researchers believe that a large majority of people in modern societies suffer from cumulative sleep deprivation, leading to waking-state accidents and lost productivity. The simplest way to eliminate sleep debt is to arrange your schedule so you can wake up without an alarm clock. Judicious use of melatonin, the sleep hormone, can help re-set the sleep cycle after periods of stress or travel.

2 – Practice meditation and mindfulness during waking life.

Set aside periods of quiet for meditation, contemplation and yoga on a daily basis, whether in your home or when outside walking, attuning yourself to your spiritual center and essence. Practice mindfulness and self-remembering in the midst of your daily work, asking yourself what the true purpose is of the activities and thoughts you are engaging.

3 – Increase dream recall.

Dreams are a potential treasure trove of insights and learning for creative expression, self-therapy and spiritual growth. But their right-brain image contents have to be translated into usable verbal, left-brain form. Have paper, pencil and tiny flashlight by your bedside to record dreams when you emerge from REM periods (without disturbing partner). Don't censor what you're recording – include even fragments or vague images – you can sort out meanings later. Make sure you're getting enough sleep – the focusing needed for recall is difficult if the brain is fatigued. Affirm your intention and request for dream memory as you go to sleep. Use of melatonin, galantamine and/or Vitamin B-6 (pyrodoxine) increases dream recall for some people. Alcohol or cannabis before bedtime decreases it for most people.

4 – Use dream incubation and divination to work with your dreams.

Asking for a dream related to a current problem/question in your life can be part of the intention or incubation as you transition into sleep. Having posed such a question beforehand will also be helpful in interpreting the symbolism of the dream. Assume that the dreams are messages sent to your personal ego-self from your Higher Self or Dream-Weaver – in response to your implicit or explicit need or request. Ask yourself how the dream could relate to your current life concerns. Notice your feeling-mood as you emerge from the dream state – and how that feeling is similar (parallel) or different (compensatory) from your current waking state feeling-mood.

5 – Consider whether your dream is related to the past or future.

Your dream imagery and story may be pointing you to the causes, origins or underlying issues of a problem or an illness or a conflict; or they may be pointing out some future possible/probable consequences and outcomes of present situations, resolutions of problems or suggested directions for the healing of illnesses. Dreams of creative activity may be visions sent by the Dream-Weaver to inspire you. Or dreams may be meant to help prepare you for something new or warn you of some approaching challenge or danger. Keep in mind that future dreams or visions don't usually come with a date-stamp attached. They provide unparalleled access to the realms of consciousness beyond the time-space world of our functional waking state reality – where past, present and future co-exist in a timeless matrix of interconnections.

8
The Dimensions of Energy and Pleasure/Pain

Some researchers have classified the varieties of altered states by the trigger or catalyst, such as a drug, or rhythmic drumming, or hypnosis, that induces the state transition. Others have focused on the varieties of cognitive and emotional contents (e. g. biographical, religious, creative) in different states. A third approach has been to focus on the subjective energy of altered states, apart from content. A 1971 paper by Roland Fischer, published in *Science,* arranged various states of consciousness on a *continuum of arousal,* or what he called *ergotrophic* vs *trophotropic* activation (roughly equivalent to sympathetic and parasympathetic nervous system activation).

The notion of a continuum of energetic arousal is consistent with the idea of stages of depth of sleep and the general sleep-wakefulness cycle, as well as the EEG brain-wave frequency bands. However, when considering various altered states, the concept of "high energy" is ambiguous. On Roland Fischer's scheme, schizophrenia and creative expression, both being high energy states, were at the same place on the spectrum, although one is hellish and the other ecstatic. The colloquial term "high" can mean highly stimulated, such as with amphetamines; or it can mean highly pleasurable, such as in sexual orgasm.

High Arousal

Orgasm
Ecstasy/*MDMA*
Euphoria/Peak experience

Mania
Hypomania

Schizophrenia
& Acute psychosis

Dysphoria

Stimulants: *caffeine, amphetamine, cocaine*

Excitement

Anger/Rage/Fury

**Pleasure
"Heaven"**

Fear/Panic/Terror

Agitation/Vigilance
Anxiety/Distress

Functional waking state
EEG *beta*

H E D O N I C   C O N T I N U U M

EEG *alpha*   Relaxation
EEG *theta*

marijuana

Tranquility

Drowsiness

Absorption trance

Tension

REM/Stage 1 sleep

Post-orgasm

Depressants: *alcohol, barbiturates, sedatives, tranquilizers*

opiates/narcotics

Sickness

GIIB

Exhaustion

Stage 3 & 4 sleep

ketamine

Depression

Oceanic bliss

Coma   **Low Arousal**

**Pain
"Hell"**

A R O U S A L   C O N T I N U U M

Conversely, "low energy" can mean the neutral low energy of fatigue, the unpleasant low energy of depression or the peaceful tranquility of relaxation.

Clearly, there is a spectrum of painful vs pleasurable, hellish vs heavenly states, that is independent of the level of energy or arousal. I call this the *hedonic continuum*. The diagram (p. 64) shows an orthogonal mapping of these two dimensions of states of consciousness, with the functional waking state near the moderate, neutral center of both continua. Notice that these two continua deal with the subjective energy level and pleasant/unpleasant feeling quality of the state of consciousness, independent of the particular thoughts, images and perceptions. (I should also point out that words like "anxiety" and "depression" are commonly used both to refer to temporary states of feeling anxious or depressed, and to underlying personality traits – the tendency or susceptibility to feeling anxious or depressed. Psychologists have separate tests for measuring state-anxiety and trait-anxiety.)

In the *upper right quadrant* we have states of increasingly high energy and high pleasure, to peak experiences of euphoria, ecstasy and orgasm. The lower right quadrant contains calm and peaceful pleasurable states, associated with of tranquility, relaxation and absorption, as well as post-orgasmic bliss. The high-energy, high pleasure states could be compared to a gushing fountain or rushing stream, whereas the low-energy, high-pleasure states are like a tranquil lake or peaceful meadow.

In the *upper left quadrant* we have increasingly high energy, but dysphoric and unpleasant states. People in states of terror and in acute psychosis have superhuman amounts of energy and may go for days without sleeping or eating. In neurobiological evolutionary terms, fear and rage are the subjective emotional components of flight or fight, adrenergic, mammalian brain limbic system activation in reaction to a perceived threat. Both fear/terror and anger/rage are high-energy states, but rage is not subjectively experienced as unpleasant in the heat of the moment, the way fear is – which is one reason why rage states can become addictive. At the extremes of psychopathology, manic and hypomanic states, though they can be devastating to a person's familial and social relations, are notoriously difficult to treat, because the person does not experience distress and does not seek help – instead they may feel energized, empowered and creative.

In the *lower half of the arousal continuum*, we have the decreasing energy states of the waking/sleep cycle, with deep sleep and coma as totally "off-line" states, neutral in regard to the pleasure-pain dimension. Pleasurable and peaceful states of meditative tranquility are on the right, culminating in states of deep absorptive trance and post-orgasmic bliss. Unpleasant and pain-filled states of tension, exhaustion and sickness are shown on the lower left, culminating at the extreme in the zero-energy, zero-pleasure state of depression: the depressed person characteristically has no energy to get up in the morning and no wish or desire to engage the activities of the day.

The physiological changes of the arousal continuum and the correlated variations in the subjective state of consciousness are subject to the circadian sleep-wakefulness cycle, as we have seen, as well as the subtler variations of the ultradian cycle. They are also subject to multiple changes due to environmental stimuli. The general level of energetic wakefulness is mediated by the reticular activating system in the reptilian brain-stem as well as by the relative predominance of the energy-mobilizing sympathetic nervous system and the associated adrenal hormones (adrenaline and glucocorticoids). In the low-energy phases of the circadian cycle, the parasympathetic nervous system, with its restorative and relaxing functions predominates, and the sleep hormone melatonin, which promotes stage 3 and 4 of deep sleep, is secreted by the pineal gland.

The two dimensions can be plotted on a time line, as seven-point scales, that can be and have been used as a self-rating profile of an altered state of consciousness. I call this the *Altered States Graphic Profile* and it is described in more detail in Appendix A. Possible correlations of brain neurotransmitter levels associated with these two dimensions are discussed in Appendix B.

Psychoactive Stimulants and Depressants

In the diagram on page 64, the effects of psychoactive stimulant or depressive drugs are shown as heightening or lowering of the arousal level, both physiological and psychological. I distinguish *psychoactive* drugs in this way from the consciousness-expanding or *psychedelic* drugs: the effect of the latter could not be represented on this diagram, since energy-levels and pleasure-pain changes can fluctuate wildly within the time-period of the state. (We will discuss expanded and contracted states of consciousness in the following two chapters.) The one exception is *ketamine*, which is an anesthetic that at lower dosage ranges induces abstract visual hallucinations while one is drifting in a dream-like haze, pleasurably dissociated from bodily aches and pains.

The psychoactive stimulants and depressants or sedatives (also called mood-regulating drugs in psychiatry), can have beneficial and even therapeutic effects, just by modifying the energy-level. Someone in a state of high anxiety and tension can experience less distress just by being able to relax and sleep with the use of a sedative. Someone in an exhausted and depressed state can feel better just by being able to mobilize their energy through use of a mild stimulant. However, with habitual use of stimulants or depressants, dependency and addiction can develop, perhaps because the normal, innate cycles of activity and rest are chronically disrupted. The internal conflicts or external stress conditions *causing* the depressed or anxious mood are not actually resolved or ameliorated by the use of psychoactive drugs.

The *stimulant* caffeine – the most widely used psychoactive plant/drug in the world – can help the central nervous system make the transition from sleep into the functional waking state. Arabic Sufis allegedly valued coffee because it enabled them to stay awake and alert for prolonged periods of meditation. Indian peasants in the high Andes have used the coca plant since ancient times to walk and work for hours, withstanding hunger and high altitude weakness. Amphetamines are used by truck drivers, college students and other night workers, including the military, to stay alert and concentrate for longer periods of time. Psychoactive stimulants enable the individual to override the normal alternation of sleep and rest with energetic activity. Such overrides cause the accumulation of sleep debt and if chronically repeated, eventually lead to adrenal exhaustion and the notorious amphetamine "crash."

There is a danger of contracted perceptual awareness from stimulant use: a college student I know took methedrine to write her finals and wrote furiously and copiously, but didn't notice that she wasn't turning the pages in her exam book, which was overwritten and illegible as a result. Another danger is that the extra energy has no constructive outlet: I remember once on a cross-country driving trip with friends, taking an amphetamine for my turn at late-night driving, when the car broke down and we had to spend the night sleeping in a field to await access to an auto mechanic. For hours that night, I lay wide awake, unable to sleep, repetitively churning over ideas for projects and accomplishments, with considerable pride – only to find in the grey light of the morning that it was all illusory and futile. Nevertheless, it is clear that the energy-boosting effects of stimulants can provide someone with chronic feelings of inadequacy and inferiority, enough of a boost of subjective confidence to easily lead to an addictive habit.

The energizing effects of amphetamine on speed and endurance of performance has had great appeal in the military forces of most countries. However, the price paid by the contracted perceptual awareness has lead repeatedly to "shoot first, ask questions later" types of situation, where "friendly fire" has resulted in tragic mistakes. The film *Jacob's Ladder* deals with a situation in the Vietnam war where the use of an experimental stimulant led to soldiers being unable to stop killing anyone in sight. This is a legendary liability in cultic warrior bands, such as the ancient Germanic *berserkers* – bear-pelt wearing warriors, who in their states of battle frenzy would kill anyone that moved.

The effects of *alcohol*, the most widely used depressant in the world, can be arranged on a dose-dependent continuum, ranging from relaxation and relief from anxious tension, to disinhibition euphoria and/or aggression, to deep sedation, stupor and death. The ancient Roman proverb *in vino veritas* attests the tongue-loosening effect of a glass of wine, as masks of shyness may be undone. The proverbial bar-room fight attests the release of inhibitors on aggression. Individual variations in sensitivity interact with alcohol concentration and speed of absorption. As learned social inhibitors on lust and aggression are depressed (i. e. turned off), cocktail party flirtations become more blatantly sexual, and verbal disagreements may become physical altercations. Sociologists studying juvenile gangs have found that violence is strongly correlated with alcohol use. Learned skills that require concentration are adversely affected, as is well known from the dangerous association of drinking and driving.

For myself, and perhaps other natural introverts, the dose-response curve of alcohol inebriation appears to be so steep that I rarely experience the wine-induced disinhibition euphoria – moving instead from mild relaxation to morose withdrawal. For the same reason, those who attempt to self-medicate their depressed and anxious state with alcohol are liable to find their depression deepening, even as their anxiety and tension diminishes. Combinations of alcohol with other sedatives, such as barbiturates, are notorious for releasing (i. e. disinhibiting) suicidal inclinations and their synergistic effect may lead to fatal collapse when breathing and heart-rate are depressed to stoppage. Nevertheless, the immediate tension-relieving effect of alcohol and the time-delay of stuporous hang-over create sufficient motivational parameters for a potentially addictive habit.

The second most popular recreational plant/drug, *marijuana*, can be thought of as mild euphoriant on the hedonic continuum and a mild relaxant on the arousal continuum. The pleasurable and sedative effect are the main components of its medicinal value in chronic pain. The main subjective effect seems to be a kind of dilation of the subjective sense of time passing – which is why it is so appealing to both musicians and those listening to music, and why it enhances all sensory pleasures from eating to sexual love-making.

As discussed above, the neuro-hormonal basis for the energy-arousal continuum is generally thought to be the alternation between sympathetic and parasympathetic nervous system activation, in circadian and ultradian cycles. Melatonin, the sleep hormone, is released from the pineal in the night-time rest phase of these cycles and adrenaline, the energy hormone, is released in the daytime active phase. As we know, these basic cycles can be and are disrupted by stress — when adrenaline mobilizes the body's nervous, muscular and circulatory systems to meet a threat by fight or flight, aggression or avoidance.

It's important to recognize that the adrenaline-fuelled stress reaction is activated by *perceived threat* — in other words, it can occur in the absence of any real, external danger, in response to purely subjective, even illusory factors of perception and cognitive misinterpretations. In addition, the attack or avoid reaction can be learned (conditioned) by association, and then be triggered by specific environmental or social stimuli, such as a word, a tone of voice, a facial expression, or by purely internal memory images or body sensations, even in dreams. Nightmares, in which we encounter the monsters and threats of the subconscious mind, are usually accompanied by adrenal-sympathetic activation (heart pounding, hyperventilation) and the arousing awareness may bring us blessed awakening ("Am I glad that was only a dream").

* * *

Suggested Exercise

See if you can identify from your own recent experience, four different states you've experienced, at different times, for each of the four different quadrants:

pleasurable high–energy (ecstatic, joyful) _____

unpleasant high-energy (terrified, enraged) _____

pleasurable low-energy (blissful, peaceful) _____

unpleasant low-energy (depressed, dejected) _____

Can you identify the set (intention), the setting (context), and the catalyst or trigger that got you into the state? How did you come out of it? Were there any lasting consequences or changes that came out of your experience in that state?

9
Expansions of Consciousness

I offer the following proposition as the essence of my argument thus far: *each state of consciousness involves a qualitatively distinct and different mind-space and subjective time-stream.* In order to fulfill our life's purpose and attain happiness, we need to learn to recognize the states in which we find ourselves and learn to navigate our way through them with conscious intention.

Besides the two dimensions of states of consciousness that I've described in the previous chapter – the arousal continuum and the pleasure-pain continuum – there is a third dimension: the *expansion vs contraction* of the field of attention and awareness. As with the other two dimensions, we are considering states of consciousness in a purely formal way, independent of content – i. e. regardless of the particular thoughts, images or perceptions that are occurring. We will consider expanded and expansive states in this chapter and contracted and narrowed states in the next.

As far as I know, it was Timothy Leary and his friend and colleague Frank Barron, when designing the Harvard experiments with psilocybin, who first used the concept of *consciousness expansion* to describe the states and the substances for which Humphrey Osmond and Aldous Huxley coined the term *psychedelic* ("mind-manifesting"). I recently learned of some correspondence, dating from 1961, between Leary and Albert Hofmann (who had discovered LSD and identified psilocybin as the active ingredient of the Mexican magic mushroom), in which Hofmann expressed his appreciation for the concept of "consciousness expansion" as applied to these drugs and states. He said that he had recently written to his friend and mentor Aldous Huxley to emphasize that research on these unusual drugs should not be limited to the pharmacological and psychiatric fields, but should include the implications and applications in studies of expanded consciousness in creativity and religious experience.

The consciousness-expanding, psychedelic drugs, such as psilocybin, mescaline or LSD, are most often referred to in the psychiatric research literature as *hallucinogenic*. However, as anyone who has experienced these states can confirm, one does not see hallucinated, illusory objects – rather one sees the ordinary sense-objects that are there, but in addition one may see or sense subtle energy-fields around objects and people, and associative patterns that one was not aware of before. In such states, in addition to perception, there is *apperception* – the reflective awareness of the experiencing subject and understanding of associated elements of context. As discussed in chapter 3, apperception or awareness of context and meaning occurs as perceptions are integrated with enhanced cognitive understanding.

This expanded awareness element, or apperception, is generally absent in the subjective experience of psychoactive stimulants and depressants, which simply move consciousness either "up" or "down" on the arousal dimension. It is also notoriously absent in the addictive state induced by narcotics, which, though it may move awareness away from pain or discomfort, is typically described as "uncaring," "cloudy," or "sleep-like."

Although psychedelic drugs do not in fact induce hallucinations, in the sense of "illusory perceptions," the term "hallucinogen" deserves to be rehabilitated. The original meaning of the Latin *alucinare,* from which it is derived, is to "wander in one's mind." Travelling in inner space is actually quite an appropriate metaphor for such experiences, which are referred to colloquially as "trips," in the psychedelic sub-culture. Any journey in subjective mind-space, whether induced by certain plants, or by rhythmic drumming, or by any other catalyst, certainly involves an expansion of awareness – as do journeys of exploration in outer geographical and cosmic space.

The most familiar and paradigmatic exemplar of an expanded and expanding state of consciousness is the experience of waking up from sleep. Whereas moments before, I may have been pursuing some activity or observing some events in an inner dream-space, when I wake up, I become aware of the fact that "I" am actually in my physical body, lying in this bed, in this room. I may look back on the dream scene I was just in, but upon awakening have now re-claimed an expanded perceptual awareness of my existence in the ordinary time-space world. My awareness and sensing may even extend beyond my bedroom, to the larger house of which it is a part, and to the garden outside, the street and other houses. If I am in a particular kind of expansive mood, I may even, with meditation and reflection, extend my awareness into the larger eco-region or city in which I am living, to the rest of the world outside, including my relations with beings and places, with family and work, with community, continent and cosmos.

Our field of potential perceptual awareness is spherical around the body – we *can become aware* of people or things moving or stationary all around us, as well as above and below. This is an experiential observation that can be verified by anyone. For example, you – the reader of this book – could choose to expand your sensing awareness from the pages of this book to include also what beings (e. g. humans, plants), things (e. g. chair, lamp) or events (e. g. radio transmission, outside traffic) are occurring around you. You may even choose to move into a meditative state, and expand the horizon of your awareness to include the community and region in which you live, and the greater planetary and cosmic world beyond.

This sphere of potential awareness is the subjective counterpart to what is called the energy-field, which can be objectively observed by others (called clairvoyants or sensitives) as well as being measurable by certain kinds of recording devices. The energy-field not only surrounds but also interpenetrates the physical body at every level – organic, cellular, molecular, atomic and sub-atomic. It can be thought of as a polarized electro-magnetic antenna system, receiving and transmitting information-packed energies of diverse vibrational frequencies in the multiple worlds of reality.

The great designer-cosmologist Buckminster Fuller (1895-1983) described what we are referring to here as the human energy-field in terms of an *omnidirectional epistemology*.

> Operationally speaking, the word *omnidirectional* involves a speaker who is observing from some viewing point. "People and things are going every which way around me." It seems chaotic at first, but on further consideration he finds the opposite to be true, that only inherent order is being manifest...Omnidirectional means the center of a movable sphere of observation has been established a priori by Universe for each individual life's inescapably mobile viewpoint; like shadows, these move everywhere silently with people. ...The inherent spherical center viewpoint with which each individual is endowed generates its own orderly radii of observation...Omnidirectional consideration as generalized pattern integrity requires an inherently regenerative nucleus of conceptual observation reference. (Fuller, B. *Synergetics*, pp. 613-615)

Fuller's emphasis on the inherent center of this movable sphere of observation is congruent with the emphasis on centering awareness, found in all forms of meditative consciousness expansion and yogic spiritual practice.

Although the field of potential awareness is actually spherical, for the sake of communication in the two-dimensional space of the printed page, we can diagram this field as a 360° circle. Let us assume that the actual focus of our attention and observation at any given point in time subtends an arc of 30°. In expanded states, perceptual awareness and attention may expand to a wider arc of 90° or 120° or 180°. This represents then a wider, more complex, range of perceptual awareness, that transcends and includes the prior arc of focused attention and awareness.

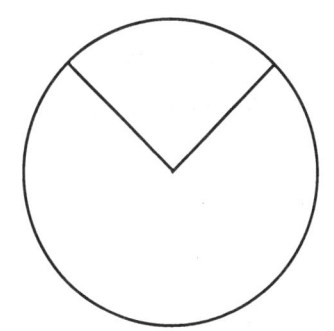

Baseline state of consciousness

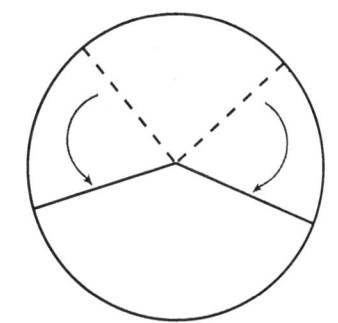

Expanded state - transcendence

Individuals who take LSD or other psychedelic, in the prototypical consciousness-expanding experience, often report that their range of visual perception has expanded to 360° — so that they felt they could see out of the backs of their heads. The biologist Rupert Sheldrake has described a whole series of demonstration experiments that verify the sensing-feeling that people sometimes have of being stared at from behind. Anyone may actually become more aware of what is happening all around them – and this is a form of sense perception not necessarily limited to psychedelic states, or especially gifted psychics.

Transcendent experiences, like the classic accounts of mystical or cosmic consciousness, involve a widening of the focus of attention, an expansion of perceptual awareness beyond the boundaries of the ordinary or baseline state. Frank Barron's research on creativity demonstrated that creative inspiration involves access to more complex, expanded states of awareness.

The *empathogenic* psychedelics, such as MDMA, produce an expansion and deepening of the field of emotional awareness, with minimal or no alterations of perceptual awareness. "Everything looks just the same, but I feel completely differently about it." A state of emotional balance or equanimity is attained in which previously painful, conflicted perceptions and memories can be experienced within a larger context of self-acceptance. This accounts for the value of empathic states and empathogenic substances for psychotherapy and healing self-exploration.

Expanded and transcendent states of consciousness generally involve some sense of detachment, a "rising above," the attachments of cravings and ego-centric desires. This is why the concept of "consciousness raising" also connotes a similar process. Consciousness-raising groups in the women's liberation movement of the 1960s and 70s involved women discussing their common interests, values and concerns, above and beyond their conventionally limiting identity roles within patriarchal family and work situations. Meditation practices, including *Transcendental Meditation* (TM), also clearly aim to produce a unitive state of consciousness, in which the conflicts and dualities of ordinary consciousness are dissolved or transcended.

In the symbolic language of alchemy, the process that most obviously involves an expansion of awareness is the operation of *solutio* – symbolized by the image of a man sitting in a vessel of warm water. Through the inner process of *solutio*, restrictive muscular armoring and obsessive emotional rigidities can be dissolved, leading to expanded and deepened psychosomatic balance and well-being.

In the symbolic language of astrology, the planetary archetype *Neptune* connotes consciousness expansion via the dissolving of **perceptual and emotional boundaries**. The planetary archetype *Uranus* points to the sudden and abrupt breaking through of limiting boundaries; and *Jupiter* symbolizes the mental expansiveness of confidence and faith.

In my book *The Unfolding Self*, chapter 1 – *Awakening from the Dream of Reality* – is devoted to the applications of the metaphor of awakening to experiences of enlightenment, liberation **and cosmic consciousness**. The importance of *awakening* from the sleep-like or dream-like ignorance and unconsciousness of what we erroneously think of as the ordinary waking state, has been emphasized by Gnostics, Buddhists and spiritual teachers such as G. I. Gurdjieff.

Several of the other transformation processes that I discuss in *The Unfolding Self* also involve experiences of expanded and expanding consciousness. In considering these, it's useful to keep in mind the distinction between a time-limited state, and the longer-term process of self-transformation and growth. In the course of a psychological or spiritual growth practice there may **be transient moments of awakening or enlightened insight**. These are then to be integrated into one's evolving understanding of the nature of reality as well as the daily life of the householder."

After the ecstasy, the laundry," as my friend, the Buddhist meditation teacher Jack Kornfield, likes to say.

In the chapter on *Uncovering the Veils of Illusion* I cite examples of experiences that were described as being like the removal of cataracts or blinders from the eyes, or distorting overlays or coverings on clear thinking. Clearly, the removal of veils or coverings, by whatever means, results in an expansion of awareness – which may at times extend all the way to cosmic consciousness. "When the doors of perception are cleansed, everything would appear as it is – infinite" was the line from a poem by William Blake, that Aldous Huxley used to describe his mescaline experiences. There is a kind of "reducing valve," Huxley suggested, that functions to keep our awareness focused on the ordinary realities we need to survive, but when this reducing valve is de-activated, so to speak, we can have access to a vastly greater "mind-at-large."

In the chapter on *From Captivity to Liberation,* I wrote about my own six or seven psychedelic experiences in a maximum security prison, with a group with incarcerated convicts and other graduate students, under the mentorship of Timothy Leary, in the 1960s.

> I vividly remember the extraordinary experience of having my visual field expanded until it become a 360-degree circle or sphere, within which the prison walls, the bars on the windows, and the locks on the door had become meaningless. Though still visible and real, they seemed ineffectual in imprisoning the human spirit, which soared unconstrained that day (*The Unfolding Self,* p. 57).

Thus I learned in an experiential, not merely conceptual way, that we can have inner freedom, freedom of consciousness, even while in an outer prison.

The converse is of course also true: we can have inner bondage, while outwardly, **to all appearances, free.** The inner prisons, shutters and locks of depressive and anxious states, what William Blake called "the mind-forged manacles," are more subtle and less obvious, and for that reason, more insidious. As G. I. Gurdjieff used to say, if we do not realize we are in prison, we have no incentive to escape, and therefore our possibility of liberation is zero. Hence the importance of seeing beyond our usual limited point of view, even if only momentarily. Sometimes a brief glimpse of the Infinite – "to see a world in a grain of sand" – can be an inspiration for a lifetime of searching.

Expanding consciousness in birthing and dying

The two most profound and radical expansions of consciousness in everyone's life occur when we are born and when we die. At birth, the emergence of the infant self from the dark confinement of the maternal womb is accompanied by a spectacular extension and intensification of seeing, hearing and other modes of sense perception. At death also, according to the testimony of those who have returned from near-death experiences (NDE), as well as the mystics and seers of all times, there is a similar emergence into a vastly expanded world filled with infinite life and light. In the words inscribed on the temple gate of the Delphic Oracle, "death comes to mankind, not as a curse but a blessing."

The parallels between these two fundamental transitions has often been remarked upon. In the words of scientist-mystic G. T. Fechner, "our death is only a second birth into a freer beingness, in which the soul breaks through and leaves behind its narrow sheath, just as the child did at the time of its birth." Yet as we know, both of these fundamental transitions, birthing and dying, are almost always accompanied by anticipatory contractions of fear and confusion, sometimes to the level of trauma and terror. The fields of peri-natal psychology and thanatology have developed precisely to help people prepare for and cope with the existential challenges of these two transitions.

In the mystical and psychedelic literature we find descriptions of psychological death-rebirth experiences, that are seen as the most profound and radical self-transformations. In such experiences, the pre-conceived, unconsciously-held self-images and thoughts of who I am, whatever it is I call "me," are dissolved or released, like clothing we no longer need to wear. After a period of uncertainty and turmoil (which in certain psychotic states may go on for some days or weeks), there is the rebirth, or re-emergence of new self-image, a new identity, that enables one to function normally in the time-space world of our social and ecological relations – but with the benefit of having had a glimpse behind the veil of death into the realms of the Immortals.

* * *

Expanding Awareness to the Possible: A Thought Experiment

When you tune into the web of life with which you are interconnected, at any and every level (other humans, animals, plants, spirits, communities, places, countries, planet Earth, Universe) you can experience the actually existing network of relations that constitute your present life-world.

Then, you can tune into the web of *all possible connections and relations*, at any level (other humans, animals, etc). This move represents an enormous expansion of consciousness, since the realm of the possible is much vaster than the actual. In fact, *the matrix of possibilities is infinite in all directions.*

10
Contractions of Consciousness

Sentience, awareness or attention can be thought of as a kind of beam that can be focused on a narrow point or band, or can take in wider arcs and areas of the total 360° circle of potential **awareness**. This awareness/attention beam changes its focus and range constantly, and narrowing or widening it are obviously normal and natural capacities, essential to safe and effective functioning in space and time.

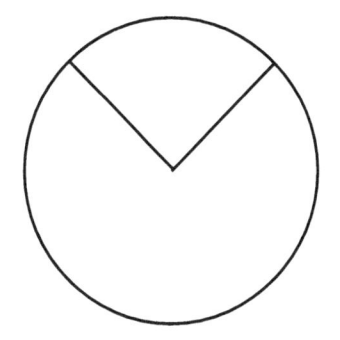

Baseline state of consciousness 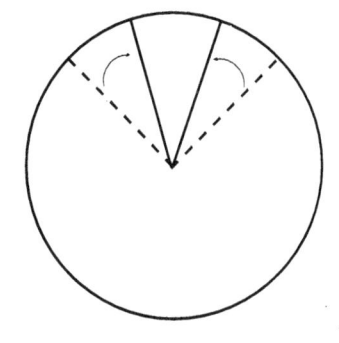   Contracted state - focus/fixation

In contracted states, as the diagram shows, attention may be selectively focused, from the baseline arc of 30° to an arc of only 15° or less. Our daily lives involve a constant adjusting, both widening and narrowing, of the focus and range of attention and awareness. For example, the reading of this book, or any book, engages the reader's focused attention. Your attention may at any time be widened again, by choice or by happenstance, to include the larger context, such as the table, the room, other people in the room and so forth. In the other direction, your attention may be concentrated even further, perhaps on a single phrase or word, or on the meaning of the concept being expressed by the word; or, if you have a printer's eye, your attention my focus on the shape of the letter in the typeface we are using…

Working on any task – whether it's driving a car, fixing a piece of machinery, creating a drawing on paper or cloth, cooking a meal, dressing a child for school, performing a musical piece, writing a letter to a friend, listening to a lecture, devising a business strategy with colleagues, planting flowers in your garden, designing a web-site, climbing a rock face, buying (or selling) an item in a store… involves a selective focusing of attention, alternating with expansions of awareness that bring in more information and complexity, and provide feedback for the ongoing activity.

The arena of interpersonal communication and relationships provides many examples of contracted, focused states of consciousness, at both ends of the pleasure-pain continuum. The ecstatic obsession of being "in love" is a classic example of such a state, in which the lover may think and sing "I only have eyes for you," while all the rest of the world is barely registered, and only through rose-colored glasses.

Sexual stimuli are notorious for their capacity to attract and contract our awareness, to the point of obsession. Sexual love-making may involve expansive states in which the physical conjunction is only one element in an experience with aesthetic, romantic and spiritual dimensions; and it may involve, in the other direction, the narrowing of "sensate focus" on the sensations spreading out from a particular erogenous zone.

Another area of human experience in which selective narrowing of attention occurs is in the mother-infant bonding situation. This was brought home to me in a very vivid way when I was watching my infant daughter and her attachment behavior toward the maternal breast. She would be moving around, gurgling and wiggling her limbs, and then suddenly she would start focusing on the breast. She would start to cry, and all her movements were towards the mother, with her attention completely zeroed in on the breast. I then lost the ability to distract her or capture her attention. I could no longer say, "Here, look at this," and have her follow my hand gestures with her eyes.

We all know how bodily pain or discomfort, from mild to intense, tends to narrow our focus of attention – as we try to interpret and cope with the body's signals of injury or illness. States of anxiety, fear and terror, as well as anger, rage and fury, are notorious for their narrowed focus of attention and perception, an observation reflected in etymology. The English word "anxious" is derived from Latin *anxius*, which is itself based on the verb *angere*, "to strangle, or tighten." This root word is also found in "angina," "anguish," "anger," and the German *Angst* ("fear"); which itself is also related to the German *eng* ("narrow"). In both fear and anger, the eyes narrow, the breath tightens and the muscles tense and contract, ready for the action of fleeing or fighting.

In fact, fear and rage may be seen as the subjective, emotional aspect of the mammalian, limbic brain, flight or fight reaction. It's easy to see the adaptive advantage of the contracting of attention in states of fear and rage: the focusing of attention on the stimulus of threat or danger helps to mobilize energy for the appropriate flight-or-fight response. We are "hard-wired" to have survival needs and strategies take precedence over exploratory interests or mystical musings — or even interpersonal communication!

Contracted states of fear and rage occur in reaction to real threats and dangers – but also, through associative conditioning, in reaction to *perceived or imagined threats*, where no real danger exists. Conditioned, fixated reaction patterns of attack/blame or defend/avoid may be triggered unconsciously (and repetitively), by a word, a gesture, or a facial mien, and lead to complex conflicts in couples, families and groups. But that is not all. The stimulus that triggers the conditioned fear or rage reactions may be purely internal – a passing thought, a memory image, a dream image – yet it is capable of activating the limbic brain system into survival mode. This in turn gives rise to the panoply of neurotic defense mechanisms, that Siegmund Freud so brilliantly illuminated.

Receptive and Active Addictions and Compulsions

Contracted states of consciousness that occur temporarily in the course of everyday life, whether due to intentional choice or involuntary emotional reactions, can become addictive habits through fixation and repetition. Whereas transcendent and expansive states involve mobility and fluidity of attention, attraction to new and different information and preference for complexity, contracted states involve the opposite: fixation, narrowing of attention and repetitive attachment to the simple and familiar. In receptive or intake addictions, it is just the object of desire, the craved sensation associated with the liquor bottle, or with the crack pipe, or the cigarette, that captures our attention, to the exclusion of other aspects reality, other segments of the total circle of potential awareness.

The comedian Richard Pryor did a performance about his cocaine addiction, which was filmed and can be seen on video *(Richard Pryor – Live on Sunset Strip)*. It is an awesome performance, in which he portrays a lifestyle that became more and more restricted, until he was isolated from all human relationships except the repetitive and ritualistic relationship with his crack pipe. He did not work or socialize or communicate with anyone -- only the pipe with which he talked, and which told him: "this is all you need." One smoke after another, and nothing else mattered; nothing else could capture his interest or attention. Awareness and attention had become completely contracted, fixated and simplified.

A useful book that summarizes and integrates social psychological research on addiction is Stanton Peele's *The Meaning of Addiction* (1985). In this book, Peele identifies the main features of what he calls "addictive experience" or "involvement." In other words his analysis is in terms of the state of consciousness of the addicted person. Addictive experiences or involvements are defined as "potent modifications of mood and sensation." This definition identifies an addictive experience as a particular variety of altered consciousness.

The process of becoming addicted thus involves an immediate or very rapid alteration of mood and sensation, in the direction of need satisfaction, anxiety reduction, and cognitive simplification. By focusing awareness and attention on the object or experience we are craving or wanting, awareness ceases to be engaged with other aspects of our experienced reality, particularly pain, fear or anxiety. There is a genuine need to reduce pain and fear, and this need is immediately and effectively satisfied. Any unpleasant aftereffects, although they may be well-known to the addict, are too far removed in future time to override the immediate feedback of satisfaction. Since the relief from pain and anxiety through the drink or drug, though genuine, is temporary, the contractive process is repeated – until psychological habit becomes physiological dependence.

The adrenaline-fuelled state of rage can itself also become the focus of an addictive process, as is recognized in the increasing attention being paid to "rage-aholism," called *Tobsucht* in German (*Toben* = rampaging; *Sucht* = addiction). If the receptive or intake addictions involving alcohol and narcotics function to reduce recurring or chronic anxiety, presumably compulsive raging, like the amphetamine and cocaine state, reduces feelings of inadequacy and powerlessness (again, temporarily).

In both the active and receptive addictions, there is a narrowed focus, a **fixation of attention**. Then there is repetition of these steps, and gradually over time, a kind of ritual may develop. The ritual aspect of addictions and compulsions is very significant. I once worked with a man with a self-described sexual addiction, that involved compulsive viewing of pornography and visits with prostitutes in which he always placed himself in submissive and degrading positions. It was extremely repetitive and ritualistic behavior — and no other kind of sexual activity or experience had any attraction for him. Even the orgasmic sexual release seemed to be secondary to the peculiar satisfaction gained from ritualistic repetition of certain symbolic actions.

The power to instantly alter one's state of consciousness, especially to move it away from painful, to pleasurable or even neutral, may generalize from the physiological drug effect to the ritualistic behavior surrounding it. For the smoker, just pulling out the cigarette and preparing it for lighting may already have some anxiety-reducing effects. Similar considerations apply in the active addictions, including compulsive sexuality (as described above), gambling, shopping or working, where the ritualistic repetition of certain behaviors in itself helps to reduce anxiety and change one's consciousness.

By becoming absorbed in a familiar routine one can avoid dwelling on anxiety-provoking aspects of life. The fact that "working hard" is an admired and admirable ingredient of the work ethic, and that obvious social rewards are associated with it, does not alter the basic dynamics. When working hard is associated with a narrowing and fixation of attention, to the exclusion of other pursuits and interests, it becomes compulsive "workaholism." Family and other social relationships may be impaired and even work productivity and resourcefulness can decline – as corporate managers have begun to recognize.

Psychedelic expansions of consciousness also powerfully modify mood and sensation, but in a way that is quite different: the entire range of experience, the continuum of sensation, feeling and perception, is extended and made more fluid. In studies by Dr. Eric Kast, terminal cancer patients who were given LSD and compared its pain-reducing effect to that of morphine, said that whereas the morphine produced a blank numbing of painful sensation, with the psychedelic they *still felt the pain but it wasn't as painful* anymore, and other more richly diverse experiences occupied their attention. Generally however, the consciousness-expanding psychedelics have not led to addiction, and narcotics addicts tend not to like them. The effects are too unpredictable, too varied, too subtle and too delayed, to allow the kind of immediate pain-or tension-relief the addict is seeking.

Nevertheless, there is some evidence to suggest that in rare circumstances transcendent experiences themselves, whether induced by drugs, or by meditation, or by physical practices such as running, can also become the objects of compulsion or addiction. If someone is taking psychedelic drugs, such as LSD or MDMA, repetitively, to the detriment of other interests, and neglect of family and other responsibilities, then you have the classic pattern of abuse and addiction. A similar pattern has been observed with some meditators, who may avoid dealing with intrapsychic or interpersonal conflict by compulsively meditating. Teachers in the Asian spiritual traditions talk about the possibility of spiritual addiction, or "spiritual materialism," and warn of becoming too attached or fascinated by unusual or blissful experiences – which are disparaged as "illusions."

The compulsive meditator or user of psychedelics may become addicted to that transcendent experience itself, so they then just want to repeat the experience over and over, which of course is not possible. There is an inherent self-limiting factor in these kinds of experiences: you can't keep transcending, you have to have something to transcend from. Or, the ego first has to build some boundaries, before theses can be dissolved in unitive states of consciousness. The innate balancing process of the organism is always engaged in restoring homeostasis.

Consciousness Expansion for Healing Contracted States

The understanding of the dynamics of contractions and expansions of consciousness supports and extends the applications of psychedelics in the treatment of phobias, compulsions and addictions. LSD found one of its principal early uses in the treatment of alcoholism. Participants in the peyote rituals of the Native American Church have been consistently successful in recovery from alcoholism. Ayahuasca, the Amazonian hallucinogenic concoction has been used successfully in the treatment alcoholism and other addictions. Ibogaine, a derivative from a Central African hallucinogenic plant root, has been researched for its use in the treatment of cocaine addiction. Psilocybin is currently being tested in the treatment for obsessive-compulsive disorders. Among the most promising applications of the empathogenic MDMA is in the treatment of PTSD (Post-Traumatic Stress Disorder) and other fear and panic conditions.

In proposing the use of consciousness-expanding substances in the treatment of addictions, I am not suggesting a "magic bullet" pharmacological cure for addiction, a drug effect to counteract a drug effect. Rather, the treatment with psychedelic substances, in traditional shamanistic societies, as well as in innovative Western therapy settings, involves a guided experience of self-confrontation, participation in shared group ritual experiences, and the acceptance of and support by a community of like-minded individuals.

Not only certain drugs, but cognitive processes that lead to expanded awareness, such as mindfulness meditation, can be used to counteract the fixations and attachments found in addictions, compulsions and anxiety disorders. Indeed, mindfulness awareness practice as the antidote to the attachments and cravings inherent in everyday existence has been a key element of Buddhist and Yogic teachings for thousands of years. Western physicians and psychotherapists have begun also to utilize meditative methods to alleviate suffering and increase recovery for a variety of debilitating psychosomatic conditions involving contractions of awareness.

The fear of death casts a long shadow over the latter parts of life for most individuals, especially those who have been diagnosed with a terminal illness. In Western and most industrialized cultures the promise of solace offered by traditional religious beliefs has waned in the light of the spread of secular and agnostic world views. Not surprisingly, programs have been developed, such as Hospice, which offer palliative care for the relentless pain of terminal illness, and psycho-spiritual counseling to counter the contractive fear of dying.

In their book *The Human Encounter with Death* (1977) Stanislav Grof and Joan Halifax wrote about their work using psychedelic tryptamines to help individuals with terminal illness alleviate their fear of dying. For individuals raised within the conventional Western materialist world view, an experience with a psychedelic substance is often the first convincing realization that their consciousness is not identical with their body, and that realms of consciousness and Spirit exist that transcend the limitations of time and space. For someone caught in the grip of a painful and frightening terminal illness, the liberation and solace that derives from such a realization is truly a divine blessing. When Aldous Huxley was dying, the old philosopher himself facilitated his final journey by partaking of the medicine (LSD) he had called a "gratuitous grace."

In recent work by psychiatrist Dr. Charles Grob at UCLA, terminal cancer patients who were given psilocybin in a controlled study, reported a significant lessening of anticipatory death-anxiety and deeper appreciation of the here-now beauty of their remaining time of life. To my mind, these studies (which were government approved research studies) represent a significant and very positive expansion of the Western medical model. It was fully understood by all participants (including doctors and sponsors) that the psychedelic drug experience was not being offered as any kind of treatment of the illness – but rather as a way of alleviating the anxiety around dying.

From my over forty years of exploration and research on consciousness expanding substances and methods, my conviction has grown that the two most beneficent potential areas of application of these technologies are in the treatment of addictions and in the psycho-spiritual preparation for the final transition. Considering the widespread fearful misunderstanding of the journey to that "undiscovered country, from which no traveler returns," as well as the increasing likelihood of massive human population reduction in our time of global collapse, the significance of such developments can hardly be overestimated.

* * *

Divination to identify and transcend addictive tendencies

According to Buddhist teachings, the roots of suffering are the relentless cycles of cravings and addictive attachments. We all have the potential for our habits of intake (alcohol, drugs, eating, sex, collecting) to become addictive; and for our habits of activity (gambling, exercising, sexuality, shopping, working) to become compulsive.

Can you identify in your own life one or to of your own habits, of either the intake or the active kinds, that are addictive or compulsive – or maybe were that way in the past? Ask yourself what function does (or did) that compulsive habit or attachment serve? What need is (or was) being met? Does it reduce anxiety or help to move you out of depressive moods? Does it elevate your sense of self-worth, or attractiveness, or power?

Can you see how the compulsion/addiction contracts your awareness and disconnects you from deeper and more meaningful relations with fellow human beings, your environment, and with Spirit? You can articulate the intention to transcend and transform these habits. Then, when you feel the urge to indulge in your particular addiction or compulsion, you can practice centering and mindfulness to raise awareness to the larger context of your life and your relations – and make different choices.

11
Dissociation and State Transitions

The transition from one state to another, including the ordinary state transitions of waking up, falling asleep, usually involve some degree of dissociation, discontinuity or disconnect from the prior state. As we discussed in chapter 3 (on the heuristic model of ASC) we say we are in a "different state," when not only our particular thoughts and beliefs, or even our moods and feelings, are changed, but when there is a distinct change in the parameters of perceived space and time, and of our sense of identity or self. The diagnostic questions asked by paramedics of someone who may be in a state of shock, are questions about whether they can orient themselves as to the time, date and current location.

We say someone is "spacing out" when describing the apparent partial loss of communicative contact of someone going through a state transition. Phrases that a person may use to describe their own state transitions include *feeling turned on, feeling high, getting off, feeling light-headed, feeling unsteady, faint or dizzy, sensations* of *tingling, chills, heat, vibrations* and the like.

Somatic symptoms observed by others in someone who may be undergoing a state transition include: whole body or face jerking or twitching; collapsing, fainting, falling down; staggering; trembling or shaking; sweating, especially around the lips; sudden rapid, shallow breathing; eyes wide open, staring; or eyes tightly closed while talking; voice changes – voice higher or deeper than usual; facial flushing or blanching. The tiny beads of sweat around the lips, the pulsing of neck arteries, the wide-eyed stare – were among the signs of trance that Milton Erickson trained himself to observe when he was guiding people into hypnotic states.

Dissociation or disconnecting is essentially the opposite mental process from association or connecting. There is a serious category of psychopathology called dissociative disorders and dissociative identity disorders, which we will discuss below, but the basic process is simple and natural. When I focus my attention and perception on some object in my external (or internal) environment, I am to some degree disconnecting from other objects and from background. On waking up we gradually, or abruptly, dissociate from the imagery and scenery of our dreams. When going to sleep, we gradually dissociate, voluntarily or involuntarily, from our ongoing perception of the room we are in, the bed we're in, the person we're sleeping with, and lastly our own body sense.

The unconscious and abrupt disconnect from functional awareness of ordinary time-space reality is particularly evident in the contracted states of fear and rage, as well as in mania and depression. Common language and psychiatric diagnosis distinguishes readily between transient states, and the frequent occurrence of such states as a personality trait or disorder. *Panic attacks* occur in those with anxiety disorder; *flashbacks* are among the signs of a post-traumatic stress disorder (PTSD); distinct, transient *episodes* of depression or mania, lasting hours or days (if not medicated), occur in those with a depressive or manic-depressive disorder.

Our common language recognizes the dissociative transition to a contractive rage state in colloquial expressions such as *throwing a fit*, *flipping out*, *losing one's temper* ("tempered" means "balanced"), *going ballistic*, or *being beside oneself with rage*. The latter expression in particular hints at something like a partial out-of-body experience occurring with rage. Here too we can readily distinguish the transient, time-limited states, from the underlying personality trait, normal or disordered. The psychiatric experts who write the DSM diagnostic manuals, are reportedly considering including a new kind of personality disorder, called *explosive*, to describe the susceptibility to uncontrolled outbursts of rage.

We may think of associative and dissociative processes in terms of the connections and disconnections of the four main strands of awareness:

ideas, thoughts, cognitive processes..........................
visual images (plus sounds, smells, tastes, etc)...............
emotions, affects, feelings ....
body sensations – tactile, kinesthetic, thermal, etc...........

Particular tastes (e. g. your grandmother's cake) or sounds (e. g. a bird's song) may trigger associated memories of beautiful childhood experiences. On the other hand, painful experiences may be recalled in one of these strands and dissociated from the others.

I have had the experience of recollecting an event that occurred on a farm in Bavaria, when I was seven or eight years old. I had the mental memory, with no particular feeling connected to it. One day, working with a memory practice, I suddenly felt the long-disconnected emotions of shame and guilt that were associated with that event. It was a bit like lancing a boil, and releasing the toxic emotional pus.

In cases of childhood sexual abuse, where negative emotional reactions are typically dissociated, the adult may remember the event mentally, as "no big deal," i. e. without any emotional charge. Only after some exploring, in a trusted therapeutic setting, can the shame and rage be safely re-experienced. Or, the adult survivor of sexual abuse may just have uneasy, anxious feelings connected with their genitalia, inhibiting normal sexual pleasure, but with no mental or visual memory of any violation. In states of anxiety and turmoil, the thinking and sensing bands are blocked, only the emotional band is churning and occupying attention.

Dissociative Disorders

In the so-called dissociative disorders, the defining feature is the loss of, or disconnection from, some part of the ordinarily multiple strands of awareness. For example, in hysteria there may be the numbing of sensation in one arm, without any awareness of how this occurred or how the sensation can be re-established. A more extreme form of identity dissociation is the (fortunately) rare occurrence of fugue states (also called *psychogenic fugues*), in which the individual may find him/her self or "come to" in an unfamiliar locale, having no memory of having travelled there, or for what purpose, sometimes even having checked into a hotel under another name.

When I was working as a psychologist in a mental health clinic, many years ago, I once was consulted by a woman, who said she didn't know who she was – that she couldn't identify with the name or picture on her driving license, or the people who knew her and called her by that name, including the man who "claimed he was her husband." What struck me was that she didn't seem distressed, in fact she maintained a pleasant, even chatty manner, while describing the puzzling loss of some of the links in her chain of memories. She seemed to be conducting her life along more than one parallel time-stream. She accepted my offer to try to help her figure out where the missing links were – but I was not surprised when she didn't come for a second appointment.

A mild form of involuntary dissociation, like fugue, is the temporary memory loss phenomenon of *jamais vue*. When driving along a familiar route, coming to a part of the road where there are no street names or signs, I may suddenly have the sense of being in a strange environment, "never seen" before. Slightly disorienting, after a brief time, the sense of familiarity returns – the efficient functioning of the body-mind has not been interrupted or impaired. The converse experience of *déjà vue* ("already seen"), where there is apparent recognition of a new perception *as if* it was already familiar, seems to involve some slippage along the time line into the future.

When the dissociation involves not only one's sense of time and space, but also one's sense of identity, the DSM-IV (Diagnostic Statistical Manual) now speaks of *dissociative identity disorder (DID)*; this was previously called, more notoriously, multiple personality disorder. While rare cases do occur where one person may be the host for two to ten (or more) distinct, developed personalities, with different names and characteristics, more commonly one finds identity fragments that are separated from each other and the host personality by what is called an *amnestic barrier*.

While all of us to some degree have multiple *personas*, the different roles and personality characteristics we manifest in different situations, what makes the DIDs different is that the *switching*, as it is called, from one identity (called *alter*) to another occurs involuntarily and unconsciously. A psychoanalyst friend of mine told me he did psychoanalytic therapy with a client for ten years and never suspected that she was a multiple – since he never saw her switch into one of her other *alters*.

It is now generally accepted in the field that dissociated identities, also called "ego-states," develop in reaction to chronic physical and/or sexual abuse in childhood. A common theme that emerges is that the child who is being repeatedly violated (most often by a family member) "goes off" in his/her mind, to some other "place," while the perpetrator is abusing his/her body. In time, one or more separate identities may develop, some of which are violently angry and resentful – but the dissociation keeps that angry *alter/self* safely away from appearing in ordinary family interactions.

A functional ego-self develops otherwise normally, but the encapsulated violent *alter* may erupt from latency into expression years later, leading the affected individual to commit seemingly unpredictable acts of horrific violence in war-time, or domestic stress. Psychohistorian Lloyd deMause is one among many researchers, who believes that in these kind of dissociated residues of child abuse, we can find the origins of violence and war.

> *Alters* are the time bombs embedded in the right brain during childhood that are the sources of all later violence. Because they are dissociated modules, the adult can seem to be any personality mode, even passive and withdrawn, but when they act out the earlier hurts and fears and rages against a Bad Self victim, they can become a murderer or a terrorist or soldier massacring…without guilt (DeMause, *Journal of Psychohistory*, 2007).

The Difference between Dissociation and Repression

It is not widely understood that the concept of dissociation is a quite different sort of psychological process than the more commonly encountered notion of repression. There was actually a split in the history of psychiatry about a hundred years ago, with Sigmund Freud and his psychoanalytic followers espousing the central role of repression, *versus* Pierre Janet and Freud's early mentor Joseph Breuer, who championed the concept of dissociation. Janet had written in his book *Les Automatisms Psychologiques* (1889) of a "disaggregation" of clusters of ideas, sensations and movements, splitting off from the main personality, for example in sleep-walking and other forms of automatic-seeming behaviors. The American psychiatrist Morton Prince, in his book *The Dissociation of Personality* (1906) had written of a "co-conscious" (not "sub-conscious") aspect of personality in such automatisms.

Stanford University psychologist and hypnosis researcher Ernest Hilgard clarified the distinction between repression and dissociation in his book *Divided Consciousness* (1977). In the psychoanalytic model, repression is one of the defense mechanisms of the ego, that hold down, or push down *horizontally*, the primitive, body-centered, sexual and aggressive drives and impulses of the unconscious *id*, which then come out only in symbolic form in dreams, or disguised form in "Freudian slips" of the tongue, jokes and mistakes. These defense mechanisms, which also include isolation, denial, projection and intellectualization, are conditioned reactions learned by the ego to deal with the fear of being overwhelmed by so-called primal, instinctual impulses.

In dissociation by contrast, as Hilgard explains, there is a *vertical splitting* of layers of conscious, pre-conscious and unconscious contents, including primal, instinctual impulses and feelings, but also thought-forms and images, and functional capabilities of managing relations with external reality.

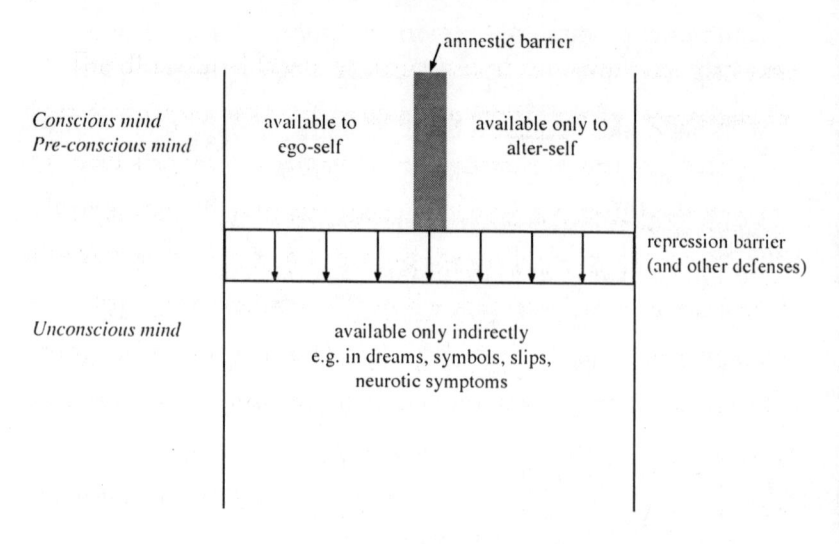

```
                          amnestic barrier
                               ↓
Conscious mind        available to    │    available only to
Pre-conscious mind     ego-self       │      alter-self
                                      │
─────────────────────↓─↓─↓─↓─↓─↓─↓────────── repression barrier
                                             (and other defenses)

Unconscious mind       available only indirectly
                       e.g. in dreams, symbols, slips,
                            neurotic symptoms
```

Repression and Dissociation

The dissociated layers or structures of consciousness may have their distinct sense of self or identity; which is why researchers in this field also refer to different "ego-states." In extreme forms of splitting, the different ego-states may have a recognizable personality and name – which is behind the earlier terminology of split or multiple personalities. When the amnestic barrier is particular strong (as in reaction to chronic childhood abuse), these separate clusters of conscious and unconscious contents are not aware of each other; nor is there control over the switching from one parallel cluster to another.

Under ordinary, normal conditions of child and youth development, there is no amnestic barrier between ego-states, and in adulthood instead there is then the conscious, intentional switching between identities and persona-roles that one has learned to perform. For example, a man may switch easily between being (playing the role of) a manager in the office, a father to his children, a devoted son to his aging parents, a coach for a local sports team, an avid music hobbyist or collector – and other roles. A woman doctor may switch seamlessly between functioning as a mother to her children, a physician to her patients, a caring friend to a colleague in trouble, an athlete, a volunteer in a charity, an activist on a political campaign – and other roles.

Hypnosis and the Treatment of DID

The classic exemplars of dissociated states of consciousness occur with hypnotic trance, where the induction technique, or the different forms of direct or indirect suggestion function to guide the individual to deeper and deeper states of absorption, in which there are increasing degrees of disconnect from the ordinary perception of time-space reality. Thus, hypnosis can be and has been used to dissociate from pain perception, as in anesthesia; or to induce different perceptual blocks or distortions (as demonstrations); or to play-act the role of an animal; or to track the origin of painful thought-feeling complexes, as is done with hypnotherapy.

There is some debate in the literature dealing with hypnosis, whether there is in fact an identifiably different state involved, or whether the so-called hypnotic phenomena could all be performed by a compliant, highly suggestible subject – in effect pretending. In any case, dissociation is involved in the increasing focus or concentration of the subject on the inductive object or phrase, as well as the gradual withdrawal of perception from the details of the current time-space environment.

"My voice will go with you," was the phrase Milton Erickson often used during hypnotic induction, as if he was giving the person something to hold on to, as they travelled deep within the wells of their memories. But Erickson was also the master of indirect suggestion, embedding his suggestions almost casually and imperceptibly in the ordinary flow of conversation, slowing down his speech (thereby probably slowing both the subject's brain waves and his own) and sometimes slurring or emphasizing unusual words, to encourage the disconnect from the moorings of functional time-space reality.

Given the role that dissociation plays in concentration and focusing in hypnosis, it is not surprising that hypnotherapy is the treatment of choice for dissociative identity disorders (DIDs). Here the task of the therapist is to form an alliance with the most central of the several personalities (sometimes called the "inner self-helper") and through deep therapeutic trance work, bring the different strands of ego-states back together.

Dissociation in Psychedelic Drug States

The classical psychedelics or entheogens, such as LSD, mescaline/peyote and psilocybin/mushrooms are typically characterized by a vast increase in mental and visual associations, and thus expansions of consciousness, to include more subtle and spiritual dimensions. However, contracted and dissociated states may also occur with psychedelics, if the person gets caught in a repetitive thought-loop driven by fear or mistrust of others in the setting. Dissociated states may also occur with psychedelics if the dosage level is too high for that individual, so that the amplified sensations and perceptions cannot be assimilated.

It is important to realize that dissociated drug states, involving profound disconnect from time-space reality, are quite different than the classic psychotic-like "bad trip," marked by confusion, high anxiety, strange sensations and distorted perceptions. I have myself experienced a dissociative state (with high-dose ayahuasca) that I did not, at the time, experience as unpleasant and confusing – on the contrary, I was totally and pleasurably absorbed in the rhythmic chanting I was doing. Only later, by reconstruction and to my chagrin, did I realize that I had no memory of certain of my behaviors or vocalizations, or the reactions of other people towards me. Dissociation is tricky in this way: it's not that I had forgotten some of my experiences – it's more like "I" never had them, or never recorded them in memory in the first place.

There are psychoactive drug states, in which the dissociative element is much more prominent than with the classical psychedelics, even at low or moderate dosages. I discuss such drug experiences in Appendix C. In an intermediate category is ketamine, a so-called "dissociative anesthetic," which has attracted the interest of psychedelic drug researchers and therapists, as well as recreational users. In emergency medicine, particularly with children, ketamine is valuable because it produces anesthesia without depressing respiration or heart-rate.

At dosages lower than those used for anesthesia, ketamine can produce vivid, kaleidoscopic hallucinations and a sense of floating free of all bodily reference points. Some of the visual effects of ketamine resemble those experienced with LSD and psilocybe mushrooms, but the anesthetic, numbing effect is the diametric opposite of the enormous heightening of sensation found with the psychedelics.

* * *

12
Dissociation and Association in Various States

We have seen how the process of dissociation or disconnection is always involved in the transition from one state to another. We ordinarily move easily and fluidly between concentrated, focused states of mind, in which dissociation predominates, to more expansive, diffuse states, in which associative processes predominate. Within a given state of consciousness the relative preponderance of associative and dissociative processes varies. Expanded states of consciousness involve extensions of associative connections, whereas in contracted states (fear, rage, depression, compulsions, obsessions and addictions) there is progressive disconnecting, narrowing of attention and repetitive fixation. Let us examine the relative dominance of associative and dissociative elements in various, more or less familiar, states.

Functional waking state

Here we can see the inherent, natural connection between dissociation and concentration: when we concentrate on some object of sense perception (visual, auditory, tactile or inner sense modality) we are consciously dissociating from perception of the surrounding environment or context. When we concentrate on perception of a figure, we disconnect from awareness of the background. Similarly with purely internal processes: when I focus on pursuing a particular line of thought or imagery, then I'm disconnecting/dissociating from other tangential, irrelevant or distracting thoughts or imagery. In a conversational group, if I'm attending with focus to one person I'm speaking with, I'm less aware of the others; but then I may let my focus and awareness expand to take in the general flow of conversation amongst all the people in the group.

Meditative states

The relative predominance of concentrative, dissociative processes and expansive, associative processes differs in the different kinds of meditation. In the classical *Yoga Sutras* of Patanjali, there is a sequence of stages one goes through during meditative practice: there is the stage of one-pointed focus *(dharana)* on an external or internal object, and the exclusion of others; this is followed by the stage of witnessing *(dhyana)*, in which the subject and object are in equilibrium; and this is followed by the complete fusion oneness of *samadhi*. In Tantra Yoga and in Tibetan Buddhism, as well as in the light-fire yoga practices we use in the alchemical divinations, there are carefully constructed visualizations that involve concentrating on the energy-centers *(chakras)* and channels of energy-flow *(nadis)*, and disconnecting from tangential and distracting lines of thought.

By contrast, in mindfulness *(vipasssana)* meditation and Zen Buddhist practices, one simply observes the flow and movements of the breath, of body-sensations, of the stream of thoughts, and does not focus attention on any one thing. The mind may wander all over, following associative patterns, but these are not analyzed or pursued (such as might occur in psychoanalysis), but simply observed and noted. A kind of detached witnessing or observing consciousness develops, that includes, but does not select or focus on any contents.

In one Buddhist practice, you notice, as you observe the stream of thoughts, the space between thoughts – and then begin to let that space, that time-interval between the end of one thought and the beginning of the next, expand. The Dalai Lama, in one of his writings, has described this kind of meditative practice as follows –

> Gradually, in the midst of the internal chatter, one will begin to glimpse what feels like a mere absence, as state of mind with no specific determinable content. At the beginning, such states may be only fleeting experiences. Nevertheless, as one becomes more experienced in this practice, one will be able to prolong the intervals in one's normal proliferation of thought. Once this happens, there is a real opportunity to understand experientially what is described in the Buddhist definition of consciousness as "luminous and knowing." (*Universe in Single Atom*, p. 159).

Open Focus attention training

Similar to this Buddhist practice is what Lester Fehmi, the biofeedback researcher, calls *open focus* meditation. He discovered, after repeated, frustrating failed attempts to put himself in the relaxed state of mind that would generate coherent *alpha* waves on the EEG, that they came when he "gave up" struggling, and just relaxed into the contentless background awareness field. In open focus meditation, one attends to the space in the head, in the chest, in the body, between the hands, between the ears, etc – and ignores the particular thoughts, images, feelings or sensations. Gradually, a calm, disengaged, yet alert and conscious state is attained – from which one can move either into deeper states of absorptive trance (*theta*), or return into the functional, thinking and doing mode (*beta*).

> Objectless imagery – the multisensory experience and awareness of space, nothingness, or absence – almost always elicits large amplitude and prolonged periods of phase-synchronous alpha activity. "Nothing" is not merely nothing. Nothing, in fact, is a great and robust healer and is critical to the health and well-being of our nervous system. Space is unique among the contents of our attention because space, silence, and timelessness cannot be concentrated on or grasped as a separate experience. It slips through, permeates your attention, through all your senses. …When the mind is asked to imagine or attend to space, there is nothing – no-thing – to grip on to, to objectify and make sense of, no memories of past event or anticipation of future scenarios. The brain is allowed to take a vacation…cortical rhythms slow quickly into alpha, and later into theta…The imagination and realization of space seems to reset stress-encumbered neural networks and return them to their original effortlessly flexible processing. Then, after this "vacation," overall performance is enhanced. (Fehmi, L. *The Open-Focus Brain*, pp 36-39).

Absorptive trance states

The word "trance" derives from the Latin *transire,* to "move or pass across" and is related to *transit, transition* and *transient.* All state transitions, and all journeys, inner or outer, involve a departure or disconnect from the starting point (or baseline or previous state) then a passage of time in which certain experiences occur; and then a return, or reconnection to the home-base of ordinary, time-space functioning,

In a hypnotic trance, the stronger the dissociative disconnect, the longer it takes to return to the waking state. Sometimes a hypnotized subject may be in such a deeply dissociated trance that it takes the practitioner considerable time and effort to bring them back. States of shock are essentially deep dissociative trances occurring in reaction to traumatic stress, that require medical intervention. On the other hand the yogic state of *samadhi* could be considered a lucid absorptive trance, in which all distinctions and ego-boundaries are diffused or dissolved in an all-inclusive oneness. Such deep absorptive trances are called *Versenkung* ("immersions") in German.

Flow states

Absorptive trance states can also occur in the course of active, complex task functioning by experienced and practiced athletes, artists or other performers. The psychologist Mihaly Csikszentmihalyi refers to such states as *flow* – in which the performer is completely immersed in the effortless flowing sequence of actions, without any distracting thoughts or perceptions.

> What is common to such moments is that consciousness is full of experiences and that these experiences are in harmony with each other. …what we feel, what we wish, and what we think are in harmony… Flow tends to occur when a person faces a clear set of goals that require appropriate responses… When goals are clear, feedback relevant, and challenges and skills are in balance, attention becomes ordered and fully invested. Because of the total demand on psychic energy, a person in flow is completely focused. There is no space in consciousness for distracting thoughts, irrelevant feelings… The sense of time is distorted: hours seem to pass by in minutes. (Csikszentmihalyi, *Finding Flow*, p. 29/30).

It's characteristic of such absorptive, yet active flow states that (1) one is completely immersed in the experience, effortlessly concentrating and without distractions; (2) there is clear intention and commitment to attainable goals; and (3) the mental, emotional, perceptual and sensory bands of awareness are all engaged and synchronous. Interestingly, Csikszentmihalyi refers to the time dilation experienced in such states – one of the clearest signs of an altered state of consciousness.

Sexual Experience

The psychophysiological experience of sexual arousal, orgasm and post-orgasmic mergence can also be understood in terms of the balance of associative and dissociative elements. In the arousal phase, there is a gradual build-up of muscular tension in the lower parts of the body and of electrical charge potential in the deep-seated parasympathetic nerves of the abdomen and pelvis. Subjectively, as pleasure sensations spread out from the erogenous zones on the skin, there is progressive concentrative disconnect from perception of other, non-sexual sense stimuli.

The orgasmic peak involves a spinal reflex electrical discharge, accompanied by rhythmic pulses of pelvic muscle contractions, and a total dissociated focus on the pleasure sensations engulfing the entire body.

In the post-orgasmic phase, there is a switch to associative, empathic mergence, where the lovers may feel as though they are literally occupying the same body-space, or inside each other, and feeling each other's feelings or the same shared wave of feeling. Gradually, after the post-orgasmic rest-period, the individual lovers move either into the sleep state, or back into the functional waking state.

In Appendix D, I discuss recent research on the complex biochemical and hormonal underpinnings of sexual experience state changes. In general, it appears that the pituitary hormone oxytocin, a uterine contractor, is released during the arousal and peak phase; whereas the lactation hormone prolactin, which counteracts arousal and produces feelings of calm, empathic mergence, in the post-orgasmic phase.

Teachers and practitioners of the Indian Tantric and Chinese Taoist traditions of non-orgasmic love-making, as well as the related 19th century American practice of *karezza,* argue that by foregoing the acute tension and arousal peak of orgasm, one avoids the extremes of post-orgasmic prolactin-fuelled let-down, and instead continues in mild-to moderately intense levels of ongoing oxytocin-fuelled sexual affection.

The use of conscious breathing and yogic practices during sexual arousal mitigates the dissociative contraction of attention common with ordinary or reproductive sex, and instead helps maintain an associative receptivity to spiritual energies from higher dimensions.

13
NDEs, OBEs and Mediumistic States

In approaching the unusual states of consciousness described in this chapter, it's important and useful to remember William James's principle of radical empiricism. The scientific approach to these topics that some regard as marginal or paranormal (and hence beyond the pale of scientific reasoning) is (1) to gather and compare observations made by multiple observers, and (2) to separate, in our thinking, the phenomenological descriptions of human observers from our theoretical reflections on the implications of these findings for our worldview.

These experiences involve a more or less complete dissociation from the ordinary, functional body consciousness – yet they are not an unconscious coma-like condition. Rather, these states are characterized by a vast expansion and deepening of awareness into the spiritual and transpersonal dimensions of our beingness. In this chapter I will discuss what we can learn from these unusual states of consciousness, their implications for spiritual growth and the evolution of consciousness.

NDEs (Near-Death Experiences)

NDEs came to the attention of social scientists and philosophers in the 1970s with the publication of books by Raymond Moody, Karlis Osis, Bruce Greyson, Kenneth Ring, Melvin Morse and others. Probably advances in life-saving emergency medical technologies contributed to more individuals being successfully resuscitated after near-fatal accidents or during surgery. About 20-30% of individuals actually coming close to physical death and reviving, report the classic NDE after their return to waking consciousness. Autobiographical accounts of NDEs continue to appear almost every year, and regularly land on best-seller lists. There appears to be an insatiable spiritual hunger for news about the process of dying and the after-life.

In terms of the heuristic model of altered states presented in chapter 6, the catalyst for an NDE is the recognition by the subject of actually crossing some kind of threshold into physical death. This kind of experience should be distinguished from "ego-death" experiences in profound drug-induced or holotropic re-birthing states, where one may subjectively *feel as if* they are dying, when there is actually no objective indication of physiological death.

The clock-time duration of the NDE (established after the fact) can vary from a few minutes to half an hour or more. Subjectively, the time-space dimension is completely transcended, as the depth and vast range of experiences remembered and reported seem to occur in a timeless and dimensionless realm. The sense of being in a different time stream is one of the strongest indications of a profoundly altered state of consciousness. The dilation of subjective time is also characteristic of psychedelic experiences.

Common features of the classic NDE identified by researchers include: a sense of being out of the body, and sometimes, of seeing one's body from above (OBE); an abrupt cessation of pain and fear and entering into a state of profound peace and contentment; a sense of crossing a threshold, or in-between space, or entering into a tunnel with brilliant light at the end; a meeting with previously deceased family members or ancestors; meeting with spiritual light-beings, sometimes identified as angels, who embrace one with total unconditional love and telepathically transmit spiritual teachings and guidance.

Some individuals report a vivid, non-judgmental review and assessment of significant experiences of one's life, often aided by these angelic beings. At some point in the experience, the celestial light-beings may communicate that the individual is not to stay in this realm, but return to their embodied life. Often, this guidance is met with some regret or resistance, but eventual acceptance with renewed commitment to realizing a spiritual vision in one's life. This sense of spiritual commitment and the reduction of the fear of death are the two principal take-home gifts of an NDE.

The life-review vision, which is a frequent though not invariable component of NDEs, may be the experiential basis for the metaphors and myths of a post-mortem judgment scene found in many religious traditions. In Egyptian mythology the heart of the deceased is weighed on a scale against the Truth Feather of the goddess *Maat*. In Tibetan Buddhism, the death-god *Yama* holds a mirror up to the just deceased, in which they can see all their deeds and corresponding intentions, which will determine their course through the *bardos*. The simplistic Christian conception of a judgment scene where the just and the sinful are separated, as sheep and goats, with the latter condemned to eternal damnation, does not find support in any of the reported NDE life review accounts.

I have myself never had an NDE experience, although once, when my car slid on an icy road and went off a 10 foot embankment, I experienced the timeless sense of calm acceptance, in the few seconds that it took for the car to land. Another time, while climbing in the Alps with my father as a teenager, balancing carefully along a steep icy slope where one misstep could be fatal, I felt the exhilarating sense of freedom and release from all earthly anxieties, together with effortless and precise concentration on the placement of each next step.

OBEs (Out-of-body experiences)

OBEs are experiences in which one has a sense of being located outside of one's normal body, floating above it or near it, in some kind of subtle body form and being able to look down on the physical body as if it belonged to someone else. Such experiences may be part of NDEs, as in cases of serious accidents or surgery, where the person may see his body being worked on by doctors, from some distance above. OBEs can occur in the course of meditative and psychedelic states, usually without the reflexive looking-back at the physical. In sleep states, we may experience OBEs as flying dreams, as I have done, enjoying the exhilarating release from gravity's pull, also without concern for the normal physical vehicle.

The reality and validity of waking state OBEs has been debated: some believe the whole phenomenon is a hallucinatory illusion, a body-image distortion, or a kind of neurological oddity referred to as *autoscopy*. Recently, electrical stimulation of certain brain-centers has seemingly produced something like this sensation of being outside of your body. Nevertheless, psychologists who have investigated the phenomenon have failed to find any correlation with psychopathology. Questionnaire studies have shown that between 10 and 20 percent of normal adults report having had at least one OBE at some point in their lives.

The controversial question of whether the perceptions in an OBE state are veridical observations has elicited some research. The cardiologist Michael Sabom reported on OBEs in hospital patients who died during cardiac arrests (and subsequently recovered). He found several who were able to give detailed and accurate descriptions of the conditions of their body and the procedures being conducted by the surgical staff. The parapsychologist Charles Tart conducted tests in a sleep chamber with a couple of gifted subjects who were able to voluntarily induce OBE's. He was able to establish that they could accurately "see" features outside of the chamber in which they were sleeping.

Studies such as these have led parapsychologists to aver that the OBE is a "psi-conducive state" – in other words, can occur with veridical clairvoyance and remote viewing – at least in selected, especially gifted subjects. Robert Monroe was one of Charles Tart's gifted research subjects who was trained as an engineer, went on to write several books about his out-of-body travels, and developed a technology, called *hemi-synch,* in which inaudible aural beat-frequencies are used to entrain brain rhythms and facilitate intentional OBE travels. The psychic Ingo Swann, who was also skilled at intentional OBEs, went on to help develop the SRI-CIA remote-viewing protocols, as part of secret government psychic espionage programs.

Spiritual teachings and practices involving intentional OBEs

In some of the earlier esoteric literature, conscious OBE travel was referred to as "astral projection." My teacher of alchemical fire-yoga, Russell Schofield, explained that this terminology is misleading, in that we are in our astral body (also called the emotional or psychic body) when we are in the astral dimension or world, which is a higher-frequency dimension quite distinct and different from the ordinary time-space world. Instead, out-of-body travel occurs occurs by means of the *etheric matrix* (also called *etheric double*), which is slightly higher-frequency than the physical (and hence invisible), but still localized within the time-space dimension. The etheric double or matrix is a subtle energy form that encompasses the physical body, extending slightly beyond it, and also encompasses every organ within the body and every cell.

The etheric matrix body functions as a template for the infusion and maintenance of vital life-force in the physical. Distortions in the relationship between the physical body and the etheric matrix are both cause and consequence of many illnesses and injuries. Psychic healers who work with hand-directed or instrument-supported subtle energy currents, channel healing energy and vitality via the etheric double. The Greek Cypriot mystic and spiritual healer Stylianos Atteshlis (1912-1995), who was known to his followers as *Daskalos* ("Teacher"), explained that

> Every body of every existence, from the simplest to the most complex structures, possesses an etheric double, centered within the body and extending slightly beyond it. . . The etheric double serves both as the mould for the body's construction and in the preservation of the body's health. (Atteshlis, S. *The Esoteric Teachings*, p. 190)

The extraordinary life and work of this Teacher (also referred to as the *Magus of Stravolos*) is described in a series of three books by Kyriakos Markides. He spent almost his entire life in Cyprus, living modestly and quietly, doing healings (for no charge) and teaching a circle of students he referred to as "Researchers of

Truth." Among the practices he taught his students was what he called *exsomatosis* (lit. "out-of-body travel"). We all leave our bodies each night, during sleep, and travel to other planes subconsciously. The aim however is to live consciously while out of our bodies." (*op. cit.* p. 191). In other words, the practice of exsomatosis is a method of inducing a conscious, intentional OBE, based on meditative practice and concentrative skill. Daskalos would arrange to meet with his students through exsomatosis at night, for healing and peace-making work, after they went to sleep.

The notion of being able to travel and function in the ordinary time-space world in an etheric double or matrix body is also consistent with Robert Monroe's mapping of his OBEs. He described a *Level 12* dimension, the first and local environment you could explore, after you succeeded in separating from the physical. Flying dreams, in which you are in a body that is lighter than air, though otherwise the same familiar shape as your physical body, can best be understood in this way. We are in the etheric double in dream states when exploring earth-bound locales and interacting with familiar recognizable humans. (If we meet flying dragons or walk in jeweled palaces in our dreams we are clearly in another dimension, probably in the astral).

Since the etheric double is higher-frequency than the physical, it can not only fly, but also pass through walls. This idea can help us understand some of the strange happenings, such as flying off a cliff, or appearing abruptly in remote locales seemingly without travelling, recorded in the books by Carlos Castaneda. It can also help us to understand aspects of the reports of alien abductions, where a sleeping body is apparently lifted out of bed, through the walls of a house, into a space-ship, where various operations are performed (sometimes leaving implants in the physical).

Mediumistic States

There is a vast literature reporting on altered states of consciousness in which some other being – spirit, deity or deceased ancestor – "comes through" and speaks (or sometimes acts) *instead of, or through the medium of, an existing personality*. Such states can be arranged on a spectrum of degree of dissociation from the ordinary personality: inspiration; channeling or mediumship; possession states. Here too, from an empirical perspective, it is useful to separate the self-reported phenomenological description of the state of consciousness from the veridicality of the contents of the statements made.

Inspiration. Who has not had the feeling of some other energy, some other spirit, some hitherto unknown flow of positive feeling coming through one in the midst of creative activity and expression? The thoughts and feelings of the ordinary personality are still there, but not presently in the foreground of awareness. You are still in the functional state of time-space reality awareness, but there is an effortless, natural flowing of thoughts, images, feelings and movements – e. g. with a paint brush or with a musical instrument. When I was writing *The Well of Remembrance,* reading and reflecting on the stories of Odin, the knowledge-seeking god of shamans and poets, I would get flashes of insight and understanding of the myths – just as the myths described drops of the "mead of inspiration" coming down from above. I did not intentionally go into a meditative altered state – I just noticed that the insights came to me after a period of concentration on the stories and on that mythic figure.

Channeling and Mediumship. In some ways, these two terms are equivalent, with mediumship being the older 19th century term, and channeling the more modern 20th century version – which has exploded in popularity and diversity in the post-1960s period in the West. The dissociative disconnect from the ordinary personality (and consequent amnesia for the channeled communication) is more pronounced than in simple inspiration, but **also varies from person to person.** There is usually an intentional setting up of a communication setting, a trance-like altered state of consciousness during which words are spoken, sometimes questions answered; and then a signing-off with the return to the ordinary ego-state. Channelers have significantly more cortical alpha wave activity during their channeling trance, a pattern also found in other hypnotic trance states.

For most trance channels, the dissociative switching of identities, though intentional, is quite pronounced. Jane Roberts, who wrote a series of highly illuminating books channeling *Seth* (self-identified as "an energy personality essence no longer focused in physical reality"), the transition to Seth speaking was accompanied by the abrupt removing of her glasses and a significant lowering of her voice.

A medium from whom I received some insightful personal readings, had such difficulties adjusting her vocal chords for the incoming spirit-being – her voice would go abruptly very high or very low – that she eventually gave up doing channeled readings, **out of embarrassment.** The well-known contemporary channel Kevin Ryerson stated that, for him, "the sensation of going into the trance channeling state is identical to that of falling asleep – rather like falling backwards into sleep." On awakening, he has no memory of the dialogue with his Spirit source that has taken place.

Mediumistic communication with deceased ancestors was much more common in the latter part of the 19th century, associated with various **Spiritist and Theosophical** groups. In Western Europe and the US, interest in mediumship declined in the early 20th century, perhaps due to the ascendancy of the materialist worldview and behaviorist psychology. But in the Caribbean (Haiti) and South America, particularly Brazil, such traditions continued to flourish, nourished by cultural elements from Africa, and the indigenous Indian populations.

In the Brazilian *Umbanda* religion, individuals learn to go into trance to invite spirits into their bodies so that they can communicate with the spirits of *pretos velhos* ("old blacks") or *caboclos* ("native Indians"), and convey their messages and healings to others. The trance induction process occurs via particular rhythmic drum patterns, and while the medium is in trance, he or she is given a cigar to smoke. It is said that tobacco smoke helps the spirits connect again to the Earth plane, since there is no fire or smoke on the astral plane.

I once witnessed an Umbanda ritual in a small church in Northern California, conducted by a priestess visiting from Rio de Janeiro. Under the impulse of the drum rhythm a pale Frenchman seemingly changed his visage to that of an old dark-skinned Indian man. While puffing on his cigar, he would then give advice to those standing in front of him. He told me that I should let my vision roam over the landscape fluidly, like water – a beautiful Taoist image. Instigated by the priestess, different rhythmic patterns brought the entranced individuals back to their ordinary personality.

Most channelers and mediums, as well as shamans, say that in their trance states they enter voluntarily into contact and communication with a higher, more knowledgeable entity or spirit – with the conscious intention of healing and/or teaching others.

Awareness of their usual body and personal identity recedes during the trance state into the background, and returns when the trance is concluded.

Possession. Full possession states, as in Haitian *voodoo*, fall at the extreme end of the dissociative spectrum, in that there is a more or less complete loss of ordinary awareness of the body and the environment; and a sense of being taken over, voluntarily or not, by some kind of spirit or entity. There is usually no intention for the possessed individual to let him or herself be used for any purpose, such as healing, beyond the possession itself.

From a psychological point of view, one could regard possession as a more extreme form of obsession, which itself can result from excessive egotistic attachment to a vision. A creative artist, inspired by a vision, may become obsessed with the challenge of bringing the vision into his/her chosen form of expression. Some artists, Van Gogh for example, have reported that the muse that at first inspired their vision and its realization, ended up driving them or riding them into states of insane possession.

Obsessions are repetitive ruminations and anxiety- and guilt-laden thought-complexes that may escalate to the point where the individual may feel compelled to hurt themselves or others. Here we are back in the realm of compulsions and addictions, contracted and dissociated ego-states, in which the individual feels impulses coming as if from some external, not-self entity implanted in them. Some years ago, I worked with a long-time heroin addict, who described his addiction as requiring him to feed the drug to the "monkey on his back." While I appreciated his description as a classic symbolic image, in a moment of extended perception I could "see" the hairy entity crouched on his back, with its claws sunk deep into his shoulders by the neck.

The psychologist and Swedenborgian scholar Wilson Van Dusen (1923-2005), who was chief psychologist at the former Mendocino State Hospital when I also worked there during the 1970s, wrote a remarkable book called *The Presence of Spirits in Madness*. In it, he compared what chronic schizophrenics said about the voices they heard in their heads, with what the 18th century Swedish mystic had said about the different kinds of spirits with which he had become acquainted. Swedenborg distinguished higher spirits, who gave counsel and encouragement to humans who contacted them, and lower spirits, who tormented and humiliated their human hosts.

Van Dusen persuaded his patients to allow him to converse with the voices they heard in their heads – the patient now acting as an intentional medium. He found, like Swedenborg, that there were two kinds of voices: most of them were accusatory and mean-spirited – perhaps reminding the poor soul of some transgression in childhood, for which he would burn in hell for ever. A smaller number of the voices, however, seemed to be supportive and encouraging. Van Dusen's approach to treatment for these individuals, who are generally regarded as untreatable by conventional methods, consisted of coaching them to listen attentively to the helpful voices, and ignore the spiteful ones.

A similar approach to pathological possession states was taken by the Canadian psychologist Adam Crabtree, who was working with hypnotherapy to reconcile the different ego-states in multiple personality disorders. He would induce a deep hypnotic trance and allow the different split-off part-selves to come forward and articulate their grievances and needs, so they could be reconciled. In a certain number of cases, it became clear that a completely different person had taken partial control of the subject's mind. Like Van Dusen, Crabtree negotiated so that he could converse with these other entities as to their origin and agenda, while his host patient was in trance.

It turned out that the majority of the possessing entities were deceased family members, who in their own unconscious after-death *limbo* state, had started occupying a child's mind, often when the latter was in a vulnerable or weakened condition due to an illness. In other words, a possessive attitude from a parental figure to a child could, under certain conditions, become an actual spirit possession after the parent's **death**. The therapy in such cases consisted, first, of persuading the possessing spirit that they were actually dead; second, that they had no business occupying another person's body and mind; and third, that they needed to go on to follow their own destiny in the spirit world.

※ ※ ※

While the extreme possession states related above may fall out of the range of personal experience of most readers, there is an important general principle here. We are vulnerable to being controlled and taken over, to varying degrees, by feeling-states and thought-forms coming to us from others, particularly when we are in a dependency situation. Vulnerable dependencies may occur in childhood, during illness, or when there is an idealization projection toward the possessing being. Such a (partial) take-over of another's identity may originally have been an innocent influence from one individual to another with whom there is a bond; it can become, through conditioning, fixated and repetitive as obsession, compulsion and ultimately possession.

The healthy and healing response to such states is to recognize the possession and to draw on Divine Spirit as well as angelic allies to eliminate the possessive elements, from one's energy-field and consciousness. Since possession states are not regarded as real within the Western medical and psychological paradigm, conditions such as those described above would probably be diagnosed as dissociative identity disorders, with delusions. Shamans in indigenous societies and spiritually-oriented healing practitioners may utilize a variety of techniques of de-possession, always invoking their own healing and guiding spirits, to restore a healthy, open and reciprocal relationship between the individual and their divine Spirit Essence.

Appendix A
The Altered State Graphic Profile

I have developed a graphic rating scale, in which the arousal and hedonic continua are shown on a horizontal time-line, so that an individual can indicate their self-rating on the subjective energy and pleasure-pain dimension, over the course of an altered state of consciousness. This *Altered State Graphic Profile (ASGP)* can be, and has been, used to compare different states of consciousness of an individual's experience. For the individual, completing the rating scale seems to help structure the recall and understanding of the experience; during confusing experiences, it can help ground one.

The ASGP can also be used in comparative research on states of consciousness induced by different drugs, or other non-drug triggers, such as hypnosis, meditation, sound, music, breathing practices, etc. I have often asked graduate students in my classes to use the ASGP in comparing some of their own altered states retrospectively, and they found it relatively easy to do so. Research on how other pre-existing variables, such as personality, might affect subjective experience of an altered state, would also be possible with this test.

Depending on the particulars of the altered state, the time-line can be calibrated for longer or shorter time periods and intervals. For example, the individual may be asked to place a check mark at the appropriate point on the two scales, every 15 mins, or 30 mins, as was done in an unpublished study of the effects of MDMA. For some kinds of alterations of consciousness, the subject may be able to indicate his or her ratings *during* the experience. UCLA psychiatric researcher Dr. Charles Grob used the ASGP during a study of MDMA, and reported that the study participants had no difficulty in assessing their position on the two scales, when asked to do so every 30 mins or so. Alternatively, individuals can also indicate their position on the two scales afterwards, from memory of a particular experience.[·]

Each of the two dimensions is converted to a 7-point scale, as shown on the left side; 0 is assumed to be a kind of neutral and normal rating in the ordinary functional waking state ("awake & calm"). The arousal or energy continuum then goes to "alert/attentive"(+1), "stimulated"(+2), and "aroused/excited"(+3); in the opposite direction, it is

ALTERED STATES GRAPHIC PROFILE (ASGP)

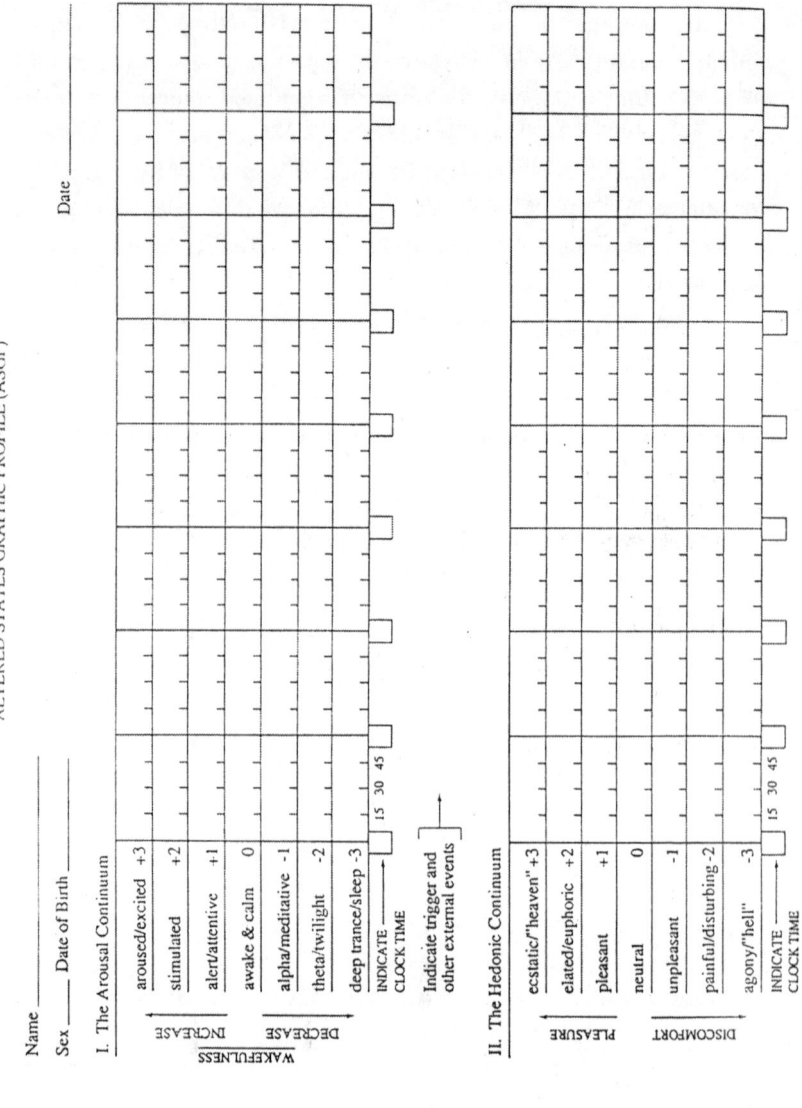

Name _____
Sex _____ Date of Birth _____   Date _____

I. The Arousal Continuum

aroused/excited	+3
stimulated	+2
alert/attentive	+1
awake & calm	0
alpha/mediative	-1
theta/twilight	-2
deep trance/sleep	-3

WAKEFULNESS — INCREASE / DECREASE

INDICATE CLOCK TIME   15 30 45

Indicate trigger and other external events

II. The Hedonic Continuum

ecstatic/"heaven"	+3
elated/euphoric	+2
pleasant	+1
neutral	0
unpleasant	-1
painful/disturbing	-2
agony/"hell"	-3

PLEASURE / DISCOMFORT

INDICATE CLOCK TIME   15 30 45

130

"alpha wave/meditative"(-1), "theta wave/twilight state"(-2), and "deep trance/delta wave/sleep"(-3). The hedonic or pleasure-pain continuum goes from 0 to "pleasant" (+1), "elated/euphoric"(+2) and "ecstatic/heaven"(+3); and in the opposite direction, "unpleasant" (-1), "painful/disturbing"(-2) and "agony/hell"(-3).

On the hedonic continuum, the negative parts of the scale would include such generally unpleasant emotional states as anxiety, fear, depression, anger, sickness and the like. It's important to note that what is being assessed is only the affective intensity and discomfort involved, not the specific emotions involved, nor the associated content thoughts or images.

The resulting graphs on the ASGP can be correlated with physiological measures such as oral temperature, heart rate and blood pressure; as well as levels of hormones such as ACTH and prolactin, and neurotransmitters such as serotonin or dopamine. Some small suggestive studies have been done making these kinds of comparisons.

External triggering events can be listed in the space between the two graphs. For example, such a list might include: ingestion of 100 mg MDMA, one glass of wine, 3 inhalations of cannabis, hypnotic induction, begin zazen meditation, begin listening symphonic music, chanting, watching sunset, etc. It is best to obtain readings of the two continua for at least an hour prior to the trigger event to establish a base-line in the "ordinary" state. Specific triggering events that affected the course of the experience can also be indicated at the appropriate point on the time line.

The ASGP may be freely copied, reproduced and used in research. The author (Ralph Metzner) would appreciate receiving reports of such uses and any studies.

References

Grob, C. S., Poland, R. E., Chang, L. and Ernst, T. Psychobiologic effects of 3,4-methylenedioxymethamphetamine in humans: methodological considerations and preliminary observations. *Behavioural Brain Research*, 73 103-107, 1996.

Appendix B
Neurochemical and Hormonal Correlates
of the Two Dimensions

In the central nervous system, the dimensions of pleasure/reward and energy/arousal appear to be correlated with the levels and activity of several key neurotransmitters – the chemicals that are released at pre-synaptic junctions, and their associated receptors at the post-synaptic junction. The evidence supporting such correlations comes from animal brain studies of the effects of drugs and the reported subjective effects of psychoactive drugs in humans. I suggest the following correlations as undoubtedly over-simplified first approximations.

It's important to remember too, that I am only discussing the possible neurochemistry of these two dimensions. In the case of the entheogens (such as LSD) there are other complexities involved in their effects (such as the multi-dimensional visions and insights) that go far beyond effects on the energy/arousal and the pleasure/reward system.

Upward movement on the energy/arousal dimension is primarily correlated with levels of the excitatory neurotransmitter norepinephrine (or noradrenaline). The stimulants, such as cocaine, the plant-extract ephedrine, and the synthetic amphetamines (which include MDMA), function to increase levels of norepinephrine in the synaptic junctions in several key brain circuits. Several classes of anti-depressants function to inhibit the re-uptake of norepinephrine, thus prolonging its action at the synapse.

Downward movement on the arousal dimension, towards relaxation and sleep, is induced by the depressant-sedative-hypnotics, including alcohol and the barbiturates. The action of depressants on brain function is mediated via the inhibitory neurotransmitter GABA (gamma aminobutyric acid), which is found distributed throughout the brain and central nervous system. Anti-anxiety drugs like Valium work by increasing depleted levels of GABA.

The neurotransmitter primarily associated with the pleasure-reward dimension is dopamine. The stimulant amphetamines (including MDMA), as well as cocaine, involve the release of dopamine at neuronal synapses (or the blockage of its re-uptake). The dopaminergic circuits in the limbic system, because they induce short, intense bursts of pleasurable sensation, seem to be particularly involved in addictive patterns of stimulant drug use. However, chronically high levels of dopamine are also found in anxiety states and schizophrenia, and some anti-psychotic drugs work by blocking dopamine receptors. This suggests some complex interactions of brain circuits that have not as yet been unraveled, and recent research suggests that disturbances of the excitatory neurotransmitter glutamate may also be involved in producing the symptoms of schizophrenia.

Because of the pain-reducing and euphoric, dreamy state induced by the opiate narcotics, they can move awareness along the hedonic continuum toward pleasure, as well as lowering the arousal level. The opiates, whether plant-based (opium, morphine, codeine) or synthetic (heroin, oxycodone, hydrocodone), exert their sedative and analgesic (pain-reducing) action via endogenous neurotransmitters called endorphins, that are structurally similar to morphine. The opiate drugs work by attaching to the endorphin receptor sites, producing addiction when these receptors are re-set to require higher inputs of external (rather than endogenous) opiates, to feel normal. Endorphins are also what enables hibernating animals such as bears to survive long periods of time at depressed levels of breathing, heart-rate and metabolism.

I have placed the effects of cannabis (marijuana and hashish) in the lower right quadrant – mildly sedative and relaxing, but also moderately euphoriant; and dilating the subjective sense of time passing, which increases the appreciation of music and sensuality. The neurochemistry of the action of THC (tetrahydrocannabinol), the active ingredient in the various plant preparations, is uniquely different from the other major known neurotransmitters. Specialized cannabinoid receptors are widespread in the brain and body – which may account for the wide variety of medicinal uses, including increasing appetite, that have been identified and documented for cannabis.

I've also placed ketamine in the lower right quadrant. It is classified as a dissociative anesthetic, used in surgery (advantageously, since it doesn't depress respiration). At sub-clinical doses it produces some psychedelic visual effects, accompanied by a diffusion of and detachment from body-consciousness. For this reason, ketamine, like GHB, has generated interest in recreational and mind-exploring circles.

The third major neurotransmitter involved with the two

dimensions is serotonin, or 5-hydroxytryptamine (5-HT), which occurs in the brain as a metabolic product of tryptophan, one of the eight essential amino acids found in protein foods such as milk, poultry, eggs and nuts. Serotonin levels are increased by the stimulant amphetamines and MDMA and, to a lesser extent, by cocaine, and also by the classic psychedelics such as LSD and psilocybin. Tryptophan and 5-HTP (5-hydroxytryptophan, an intermediate step in the biosynthesis of serotonin) are used in the treatment of depression, elevating both mood and energy-level. The SSRIs (like Prozac), which inhibit the re-uptake of serotonin, thus prolonging the action at the synaptic junctions, are also well-known anti-depressants.

Serotonin deficiency is associated with depression, and also with anger, irritability, impulsiveness and insomnia – all conditions that respond well to tryptophan and to 5-HTP. Carbohydrate cravings and obesity are also believed to be caused by serotonin deficiency, with the body trying to make up the deficit by eating carbohydrate-rich foods, which help make tryptophan available in the brain: hence intake of 5-HTP is one of the most effective ways to reduce weight. (There is also a serious neurological syndrome associated with excessive serotonin levels in the brain. While this can occur with certain drug combinations and is potentially life-threatening, it appears to be much less common than the serotonin deficiency believed to underlie both depression and anger as ongoing conditions.)

My speculative hypothesis is that serotonin functions as a mood modulator, raising the subjective energy-arousal level in states of depression and lowering it in anger/irritability. Adequate levels of serotonin in the brain may be the key to emotional balance and equanimity, allowing individuals to make more reasonable choices and reducing emotional reactivity.

In the case of MDMA, for which I coined the term empathogenic ("empathy-generating") in its subjective effects, the serotonin enhancing effect may be the basis of the calm, non-anxious, emotional balance that is particularly valuable in the therapeutic treatment of interpersonal conflict, trauma and PTSD. The dopamine releasing effect, which the other amphetamines also have, probably accounts for its role as *Ecstasy*, the drug of choice at hours-long dance parties with pulsing music, known as "raves." In addition, the presence of MDMA in the body triggers the release of prolactin – the hormone released during mother-infant bonding and breast-feeding – perhaps the paradigmatic example of empathic, non-striving, relaxed empathic mergence of two beings.

Most of the presently known psychedelic, hallucinogenic or entheogenic compounds, whether occurring in plants or synthesized, belong to one of two chemical "families": the phenethylamines (which include mescaline, peyote cactus, San Pedro cactus, MDA, MDMA or Ecstasy and others) and the tryptamines (which include DMT, psilocybin, ayahuasca, LSD, bufotenine and others). Of the four main neurotransmitters (norepinephrine, acetylcholine, serotonin and dopamine), all of the known psychedelics act strongly, though not exclusively, on serotonin receptors. The phenethylamines (e. g. MDMA) in addition affect norepinephrine, which is the neurotransmitter mostly involved with the effects of stimulants such as amphetamine (which is also a phenethylamine). This probably accounts for the more energized, stimulating properties of the phenethylamines as compared to the tryptamines. On the level of subjective experience this can be observed if one compares the extremely rapid, almost percussive beat of the typical peyote chants, with the more sedate, mellow and melodic spirit healing songs sung by *ayahuasqueros* and mushroom *curanderas* like Maria Sabina.

Research in the last couple of decades has extended scientific understanding of the complexity and pervasiveness of serotonin in the human brain and nervous systems. The neural circuits primarily involved in the biosynthesis of serotonin are found in the raphe nuclei of the brainstem, from where serotonergic neurons have projections to all other parts of the brain. The brainstem is called the reptilian brain in Paul McLean's tri-une brain model. Serotonin has also been found to be the main neurotransmitter for the enteric nervous system, a system of 100 million neurons distributed in and around the intestinal tract. This brain system is almost completely independent of the cerebral cortex. It is thought to be evolutionarily the oldest part of our nervous system.

My speculation is that the role of serotonin in this reptilian brain system, and the possible effects of psychedelic drugs in it, may be the basis for experiences of evolutionary remembering, heightened instinctual or "gut-level" knowledge, and the healing of psychosomatic disturbances possible with psychedelics.

Dimethyltryptamine (DMT), an extremely powerful hallucinogen, chemically closely related to serotonin, is found in several shamanic entheogenic plant preparations and endogenously in the human brain.

DMT is synthesized in the brain's pineal gland. Some have speculated that DMT or one of its derivatives might be responsible for the vivid imagery of dreams and spontaneous visions. Rick Strassman, who completed an extensive psychiatric research project with DMT, which he calls the "Spirit Molecule," suggests that pineal-produced DMT is released in near-death experiences and other mystical revelations.

References

Callaway, J. C. Phytochemistry and Neuropharmacology of Ayahuasca. In Metzner, R. (ed.) *Sacred Vine of Spirits – Ayahuasca.* Rochester, VT: Park Street Press, 94-116. 2006.

Grob, C. MDMA research: preliminary investigations with human subjects. *International Journal of Drug Policy* 9, 119-124, 1998.

Holland, J. (ed.) *Ecstasy: The Complete Guide.* Rochester, VT: Park Street Press, 2001.

Murray, M. *5-HTP - The Natural Way to Overcome Depression, Obesity and Insomnia.* NY: Bantam Books, 1998.

Nichols, D. E. Hallucinogens. *Pharmacology & Therapeutics* 101, 131-181, 2004.

Presti. D. E. Psychoactive drugs and the chemistry of the brain and mind. In *Encyclopedia of Brain and Behavior, Vol 4.* (Ramachandran, V. S. (ed.). Academic Press 75-82. 2002.

Presti, David and Nichols, David. Biochemistry and Neuropharmacology of Psilocybin Mushrooms. In Metzner, R. (ed.) *The Sacred Mushroom of Visions – Teonanácatl.* Rochester, VT: Park Street Press, 2005. 93-112.

Strassman, Rick. *DMT- The Spirit Molecule.* Rochester, VT: Park Street Press, 2001.

Note: The author wishes to thank David Presti, Ph. D. for reviewing the factual technical information presented in this Appendix; though he is not responsible for my psychopharmacological speculations.

Appendix C
Dissociative Drug States

The state induced by anesthetics and sedative-hypnotics involves a generalized disconnect from the functional waking state awareness of time and space. In the brain, the general depression of activity is mediated by the inhibitory neurotransmitter GABA (gamma-amino-butyric acid), and most of the sedative-hypnotics are believed to exert their effects by interacting with GABA receptors.

A recent discovery is *GHB* (gamma-hydroxy-butyric acid), which produces profound stage 3 and 4 sleep state, and has therefore found a use in the treatment of narcolepsy – where insufficient night-sleep can cause sudden collapse in the day-time. Recreational users have discovered that at lower dosages, GHB produces a profound relaxation of smooth muscles, thereby heightening sexual-sensual experience. Predictably, this has led to its exploitation and abuse in combination with alcohol, as a so-called "date-rape" drug, and its classification as a Schedule I prohibited substance.

The *opiate* analgesic drugs discussed above, such as morphine, codeine and heroin, specifically disconnect the person from awareness of pain sensations, also slowing the breath, producing relaxation and dissociating perception from the environment.

Nitrous oxide is a gas used in dentistry and medicine for its anesthetic and analgesic properties. In the 19th century the discovery of its unusual psychoactive properties attracted the attention of the philosopher William James among others. Users characterize the experience as interesting and significant, as well as pleasurable – though they are often unable to bring back any insights that hold up in the light of reason. In the 19th century, carnival-like public demonstrations of what was called "laughing gas" were held; and it continues to attract the interest of some recreational users. In terms of brain chemistry, nitrous oxide acts as an antagonist at the NMDA-type of glutamate receptor.

Glutamate is the major excitatory neurotransmitter of the brain, important in learning and memory. Besides nitrous oxide the dissociative anesthetics *ketamine* and *PCP* also function as NMDA-glutamate antagonists. As described in chapter 11, ketamine (as well as PCP) at sub-clinical doses, can cause visual hallucinations, somewhat reminiscent of LSD-like patterns, but with accompanying marked disconnect from sensory awareness of the physical body. Some researchers are now investigating whether neurotransmitter interactions with glutamate receptors may be responsible for the hallucinations of schizophrenia.

Plant extracts from the solanaceous night-shade family (henbane, scopolamine, datura), were notoriously used by shamanic practitioners of witchcraft in the European Middle Ages. They also act by inducing a strong dissociation from ordinary awareness of the body and environment, which may then lead to out-of-body visionary states such as flying through the air. In South American indigenous tribes, the healers *(curanderos)* will sometimes use datura plant extracts for diagnosing, especially in cases of sorcery; but will typically take a lower dose, and also have an assistant watching over them, in case they get disoriented. Among the Chumash Indians of Southern California, preparations from the local datura plant were used in adolescent initiation ceremonies, marking the transition from childhood to adult.

References

Dean, W. Morgenthaler, J. and Fowkes, S. W. *GHB – The Natural Mood Enchancer.* Petaluma, CA: Smart Publications, 1997.

Heiser, C. B. *The Fascinating World of Nightshades.* New York: Dover Publications, 1969,1987.

Jansen, K. *Ketamine: Dreams and Realities.* Sarasota, FL: MAPS, 2001

Pendell, D. *Pharmakopoeia. Plant Power, Poisons and Herbcraft.* San Francisco: Mercury House, 1995.

Pendell, D. *Pharmacodynamis. Stimulating Plants, Potions & Herbcraft.* San Francisco: Mercury House, 2002.

Pendell, D. *Pharmacognosis. Plant Teachers and the Poison Path.* San Francisco: Mercury House, 2005.

Schultes, R. E. & Hofmann, A. *Plants of the Gods.* Rochester, N. Y. : Inner Traditions International, 1992.

Appendix D
Biochemical and Hormonal Basis of Sexual Experience

The complex biochemical interactions of hormone levels and neurotransmitters in the brain involved in the state changes of sexual experience are still being unraveled by research. Some believe that the underlying level of libido or lust, in both men and women is a function of the balance of androgens and estrogens, weighted in favor of androgens in men, and in favor of estrogens in women. Levels of dopamine, the neurotransmitter on the pleasure dimension, rise during arousal and climax, and decline shortly thereafter.

During the arousal phase and orgasm phase, oxytocin is released from the pituitary and the hypothalamus. Physiologically, oxytocin release occurs in association with pelvic contractions (during sex and childbirth), and with sucking on the woman's nipple (during sex and lactation). Oxytocin inhibits the release of the adrenocorticotropic hormone and cortisol; in other words it inhibits the adrenal stress response. Conversely, as is well known, anxiety and stress inhibit or block sexual arousal. Synthetic analogues to oxytocin are used to induce labor in childbirth, stimulating uterine contractions. Formerly, ergotamine, an alkaloid of the ergot fungus (and precursor of LSD), was used in childbirth for its effect on uterine contractions.

Psychologically, a rise in oxytocin is associated with increasing sexual arousal and climax, as well as with feelings of trust, affection, bonding behavior, reduced fear, and healthy boundary setting; colloquially, it has been called the "cuddle hormone." Some memory functions are impaired by oxytocin, which is consistent with the dissociative effect of arousal and orgasm. Since rhythmic pelvic muscle contractions occur both during childbirth and during orgasm, mediated by oxytocin, this **raises the possibility of orgasmic birthing.** This has been reported anecdotally, and documented in films made by the Russian conscious water birthing collective.

In the post-orgasmic phase, both oxytocin and dopamine levels decline precipitately and prolactin is released from the pituitary. Prolactin is a hormone released in mother and child during nursing. Prolactin's association with the post-orgasmic phase may be the reason for the arousal refractory period in both men and women. Prolactin appears to be the hormone of empathic, post-orgasmic mergence, when there is no feeling or desire for further sexual arousal. It is a more associative period, when lovers may quietly snuggle in a peaceful unitive state, like that of mother and infant. This may also explain the pervasive use of baby talk with each other by lovers.

Researchers at the University of Hanover medical school, and elsewhere, have shown that the experience of the empathogenic MDMA is also associated with a rise in prolactin levels, similar to the post-orgasmic state. Interestingly, MDMA is also found, by most subjects, to not stimulate sexual lust or arousal (actually inhibiting erection in most men); although feelings of warmth along with sensual touching and caressing are common. Some believe that the evolutionary function of prolactin is to shift the lover's attention and motivation to non-sexual activities – nursing and food preparation in women, hunting and other kinds of planned activities in men.

References

Adamson, S. (aka Metzner, R.) (ed). *Through the Gateway of the Heart*. San Francisco: Four Trees Publications. 1985.

Passie, T. , Hartmann, U. , Schneider, U. , Emrich, H. , Krüger, T. Ecstasy (MDMA) mimics the post-orgasmic state: impairment of sexual drive and function during acute MDMA-effects may be due to increased prolactin secretion. *Medical Hyotheses*, **64 (5)** 899-903, 2005.

Robinson, M. *Cupid's Poisoned Arrow: From Habit to Harmony in Sexual Relationships.* Berkeley: North Atlantic Books, 2009 .

Birth as We Know It. 80 min documentary on the Russian spiritual water-birth processes. Directed and with commentary by Elena Vladimirova. www. birthintobeing. com.

References and Select Bibliography

Preface

Adamson, Sophia. (editor, aka Ralph Metzner.) *Through the Gateway of the Heart.* San Francisco: Four Trees Publications, 1985.

Metzner, R. **Learning Theory and the Therapy of Neurosis.** *British Journal of Psychology Monograph Supplements,* **33.** Cambridge University Press, 1961.

Metzner, R. *The Ecstatic Adventure* (editor) NY: Macmillan, 1968.

Metzner, R. *Sacred Mushroom of Visions – Teonanácatl* (editor) Rochester, VT: Park Street Press, 2005.

Metzner, R. *Sacred Vine of Spirits – Ayahuasca.* (editor) Rochester, VT: Park Street Press, 2006.

One – Altered States

Cardeña, E. Lynn, S. J. & Krippner, S. (editors). *Varieties of Anomalous Experience.* Washington, D. C. : American Psychological Association, 2000.

Hunt. H. *On the Nature of Consciousness : Cognitive, Phenomenological, and Transpersonal Perspectives.* Yale University Press, 1995.

Metzner, R. States of Consciousness and Transpersonal Psychology. In: Vallee, R. & Halling, S. (editors), *Existential and Phenomenological Perspectives in Psychology.* NY: Plenum Press, 1989.

Tart, C. T. *States of Consciousness.* NY: E. P. Dutton, 1975.

Two – Consciousness, Space and Time

Combs, A. , Germine, M. & Goertzel, B. (editors) *Mind in Time – The Dynamics of Thought, Reality and Consciousness.* Cresskill, NJ: Hampto Press, 2004.

Fehmi, Les and Robbins, Jim. *The Open Focus Brain – Harnessing the Power of Attention to Heal Mind and Body.* Boston: Trumpeter, 2007.

Metzner, R. The Place and the Story. Ch. 11 in: *Green Psychology.* Rochester, VT: Park Street Press, 1999.

Nalimov, V. V. *Realms of the Unconscious*: *The Enchanted Frontier.* Philadelphia: ISI Press, 1982.

Shanor, K. N. (editor) *The Emerging Mind.* Los Angeles: Renaissance Books, 1999.

Three – Consciousness as Context and Subjectivity

Damasio, A. *Descartes' Error: Emotion, Reason, and the Human Brain.* NY: Harper Collins, 1994.

LeDoux, J. *The Emotional Brain: The Mysterious Underpinnings of Emotional Life.* NY: Simon and Schuster, 1996.

MacLean, P. *The Triune Brain in Evolution: Role in Paleocerebral Functions.* NY: Plenum Press, 1990.

Pfeiffer, R. & Mack, J. D. (editors) *Mind Before Matter – Visions of a New Science of Consciousness.* Winchester, UK: O Books, 2007.

Four – Radical Empiricism

Harman, W. & Clark, J. (editors) *New Metaphysical Foundations of Modern Science.* Sausalito, CA: Institute of Noetic Sciences, 1994.

James, W. *Essays in Radical Empiricism.* Lincoln, NE: University of Nebraska Press, 1912/1996.

Tart, C. T. States of consciousness and state-specific sciences. *Science,* **176:** 1203-1210. 1972.

Taylor, E. (editor) *William James on Exceptional Mental States – The 1896 Lowell Lectures.* Amherst, MA: University of Massachusetts Press, 1984.

Five – States, Stages and Levels of Consciousness

Capra, F. *The Web of Life – A New Scientific Understanding of Living Systems.* NY: Anchor Books/Doubleday, 1996.

Fechner, G. T. The Little Book of Life After Death (1835). in: *Journal of Pastoral Counseling,* XXVII, 1992.

Hilgard, E. R. Consciousness in psychology. *Annual Rev. of Psychology,* **31,** 1-26, 1980.

Laszlo, E. *The Connectivity Hypothesis – Foundations of an integral science of quantum, cosmos, life, and consciousness.* Albany, NY: SUNY Press, 2003.

Macy, J. *Mutual Causality in Buddhism and General Systems Theory.* Albany, NY: SUNY Press, 1991.

Metzner, R. Stages of the Life Cycle. Ch 6 in: *Alchemical Divination.* Berkeley, CA: Regent Press & Green Earth Foundation, 2009.

Six – The Set and Setting Model

Hunt, H. T. & Chefurka, C. M. A test of the psychedelic model of altered states of consciousness. *Archives of General Psychiatry*, **33**, 867-876. 1976.

Leary, T. , Litwin, G. & Metzner, R. Reactions to Psilocybin Administered in a Supportive Environment. *Journal of Nervous and Mental Diseases*, **137**, 561-573, 1963.

Metzner, R. Psychedelic, Psychoactive and Addictive Drugs and States of Consciousness. In: Earlywine, M. (editor) *Mind-Altering Drugs*. 25-48. Oxford University Press, 2005.

Seven – Waking, Sleeping, Dreaming, Meditating

Dement, W. & Vaughan, C. *The Promise of Sleep*. NY: Dell Trade Paperbacks, 1999.

LaBerge, S. & Rheingold, H. *Exploring the World of Lucid Dreaming*. NY: Ballantine Books, 1990.

Moss, R. *Conscious Dreaming*. NT: Crown Trade Paperbacks, 1996.

Osowiec, D. Yogic Breathwork and Ultradian Hypnosis. In: Leskowitz, E. (editor) *Transpersonal Hypnosis*. Boca Rotan, FL: CRC Press, 2000.

Rossi, E. *The 20-Minute Break*. Phoenix, AZ: Zeig, Tucker & Co. , 1991.

Wangyal, T. Rinpoche. *The Tibetan Yogas of Dream and Sleep*. Ithaca, NY: Snow Lion Publications. 1998.

Ullman, M. & Krippner, S. *Dream Telepathy*. Baltimore, MD: Penguin Books, 1974.

Wise, A. *Awakening the Mind – A Guide to Mastering the Power of Your Brainwaves*. NY: Tarcher/Putnam. 2002.

Eight – The Dimensions of Energy and Pleasure-Pain

Fischer, R. A cartography of the ecstatic and meditative states. *Science*, **174**, 897-904. 1971.

Julien, R. *A Primer of Drug Action*. San Francisco: W. H. Freeman & Co. , 1995.

Pendell, D. *Pharmakopoeia*. SF: Mercury House, 1995.

Pendell, D. *Pharmakodynamis*. SF: Mercury House, 2002.

Siegel, R. K. *Intoxication*. NY: E. P. Dutton, 1989.

Weil, A. & Rosen, W. *From Chocolate to Morphine*. Boston: Houghton–Mifflin, 1983.

Nine – Expansions of Consciousness

Grob, C. S. (editor) *Hallucinogens – A Reader*. NY: Jeremy P. Tarcher/Putnam, 2002.

Beath, A. *Consciousness in Action – The Power of Beauty, Love and Courage in a Violent Time*. NY: Lantern Books/Booklight Inc. 2005.

Dass, Ram & Metzner, R. *Birth of a Psychedelic Culture*. Santa Fe, NM: Synergetic Press, 2009.

Forte, R. (editor) *Entheogens and the Future of Religio*. San Francisco: Council on Spiritual Practices, 1997.

Fuller, R. B. *Synergetics – Explorations in the Geometry of Thinking*. NY: Macmillan Publishing Co. 1975.

Holland, J. (ed.) *Ecstasy: The Complete Guid*. Rochester, VT: Park Street Press, 2001.

Metzner, R. *The Unfolding Self*. Novato, CA: Origin Press, 1998.

Sheldrake, R. *The Sense of Being Stared At*. London: Hutchinson, 2003.

Ten – Contractions of Consciousness

Grof, S. & Halifax, J. *The Human Encounter with Death*. NY: E. P. Dutton, 1977.

Grof, S. *The Ultimate Journey: Consciousness and the Mystery of Death*. Ben Lomond, CA: MAPS, 2006.

Grob, C. S. The use of psilocybin in patients with advanced-cancer and existential anxiety. In: Winkelman, M. J. & Roberts, T. B. (eds.) *Psychedelic Medicine: New Evidence for Hallucinogenic Substances as Treatments, Vol. 1*. Westport, Conn: Praeger pp. 205-216. 2007.

Halpern, J. The Use of Hallucinogens in the Treatment of Addiction. *Addiction Research*. **4 (2)**, 177-189. 1996.

Metzner, R. Addiction and Transcendence as Altered States of Consciousness. *Journal of Transpersonal Psychology*, **26 (1)**, 1-17, 1994.

Metzner, R. Hallucinogenic Drugs and Plants in Psychotherapy and Shamanism. *Journal of Psychoactive Drugs*. **30 (4)**, 333-341. 1998.

Metzner, R. Using MDMA in Healing, Psychotherapy and Spiritual Practice. In: Holland, J. (editor) *Ecstasy: the Complete Guide* Rochester, VT: Park Street Press, 2001.

Peele, S. *The Meaning of Addiction*. Lexington, MA: D. C. Heath & Co., 1985.

Eleven – Dissociation and State Transitions

Crabtree, A. Dissociation and Memory: A Two-Hundred Year Perspective. *Dissociation.* **V (3)**, 150-154, 1992.

DeMause, L. The Psychology and Neurobiology of Violence. In: *Journal of Psychohistory.* **35(2)**, 2007.

Hilgard, E. *Divided Consciousness: Multiple Controls in Human Thought and Action.* NY: Wiley Publishing, 1977.

Leskowitz, E. (editor) *Transpersonal Hypnosis.* Boca Raton, FL: CRC Press, 2000.

Putnam, F. W. *Dissociation in Children and Adolescents.* NY: The Guilford Press, 1997.

Putnam, F. & Shanor, K. States of Consciousness from Infancy to Nirvana. In: Shanor, K. *The Emerging Mind.* Los Angeles: Renaissance Books, 1999.

Richards, D. Dissociation and Transformation. *Journal of Humanistic Psychology,* **30 (3)**, 54-83, 1990.

Twelve – Association and Dissociation in Various States

Anand, M. *The Art of Sexual Ecstas.* Los Angeles: Jeremy P. Tarcher, 1989.

Chia, M. & M. *The Multi-Orgasmic Couple.* HarperSanFrancisco. 2000.

Csikszentmihalyi, M. *Finding Flow.* NY: Basic Books, 1997.

Dalai Lama. *The Universe in a Single Atom.* NY: Broadway Books, 2005.

Fehmi, L. & Robbins, J. *The Open-Focus Brain.* Boston: Trumpeter Books, 2007.

Goleman, D. *Varieties of Meditative Experience.* NY: E. P. Dutton, 1977.

Lynn, S. J. & Rhue, J. W. (eds.) *Dissociation - **Clinical and Theoretical Perspective.*** NY: Guilford Press, 1994.

Taimni, I. K. *The Science of Yoga.* Wheaton, Ill: Theosophical Publishing House, 1961.

Thirteen – NDE, OBE and Mediumistic States

Atteshlis, S. *The Esoteric Teachings – A Christian Approach to Truth.* Stravolos, Cyprus: The Stoa Series. 1992.

Atwater, P. *Coming Back to Life.* NY: Ballantine Books, 1988.

Crabtree, A. *Multiple Man: Explorations in Possession and Multiple Personality.* NY: Praeger, 1985.

Moody, R. *The Light Beyond.* NY: Bantam Books, 1988.

Gabbard, G. & Twemlow, S. W. *With the Eyes of the Mind. An Empirical Analysis of Out-of-Body States.* NY: Praeger Publishers, 1984.

Klimo, J. *Channeling.* Berkeley, CA: North Atlantic Books, 1998.

Leland, K. . *Otherworld. A Field Guide to Nonphysical Reality for the Out-of-Body Traveler.* Charlottesville, VA: Hamptom Roads, 2001.

Markides, K. *The Magus of Stravolo.* London/New York: Arcana Books, 1985.

Markides, K. *Homage to the Sun.* New York/London: Arcana Books, 1987.

Monroe, Robert. *Journeys Out of the Body.* Garden City, NJ: Doubleday, 1971.

Monroe, Robert. *Far Journeys.* Garden City, NJ: Doubleday. 1985.

Ring, K. *The Omega Project. Near-Death Experiences, UFO Encounters and Mind at Large.* NY: William Morrow, 1992.

Ring, K. & Valarino, E. E. *Lessons from the Light.* Portsmouth, NH: Moment Point Press, 1998.

Roberts, J. *Seth Speaks.* NY: Bantam, 1974.

Roberts, J. *The Seth Material.* NY: Bantam, 1976.

Van Dusen, W. *The Presence of Other Worlds: Findings of Emmanuel Swedenborg.* NY: Perennial/Harper& Row, 1974.

Green Earth Foundation
Harmonizing Humanity with Earth and Spirit

The Green Earth Foundation is an educational and research organization dedicated to the healing and harmonizing of the relationships between humanity and the Earth, through a recognition of the energetic and spiritual interconnectedness of all life-forms in all worlds. Our strategic objectives are to help bring about changes in attitudes, values, perceptions, and worldviews that are based on ecological balance and respect for the integrity of all life. Our areas of research interest include consciousness studies, shamanism and Earth mythology, and green and ecopsychology. Green Earth Foundation also sponsors the *Metzner Alchemical Divination*® training program.

Green Earth Founation
is producing and co-publishing a new series of books
by Ralph Metzner, Ph.D. –

THE ECOLOGY OF CONSCIOUSNESS

1. The Expansion of Consciousness
2. The Roots of War and Domination
3. Alchemical Divination
4. Mind Space and Time Stream
5. The Psychology of Incarnation, Birth and Death
6. Worlds Within and Worlds Beyond
7. The Six Life-Paths of the Human Soul

The Green Earth Foundation is a 501(c)(3) non-profit, educational and research organization. P.O. Box 327, El Verano. CA 95433.
Internet: www.greenearthfound.org

Alchemical Divination

The *Metzner Alchemical Divination*® training program consists of three, modular 5-day workshops, in which one learns the divinations for oneself, and how to conduct them for others.

Janus and the Gateway of the Heart

- Mapping your Self-System and Life-World of Relations
- Finding your Orientation and Inner Direction
- Releasing Fear Blocks on Receiving and Expressing
- Connecting and Reconciling with your Ancestors and Elders
- The Six Archetypal Life-Paths of the Human Soul

Hermes and the Vessel of Transformation

- Mapping your Self-System and Life-World of Relations
- Relationship Disentanglement Divination
- Envisioning Possible/Probable Futures
- Reconciling with the Inner Enemy or Shadow
- Medicine Wheel of the Life Cycle

Mimir and the Well of Memory

- Mapping your Self-System and Life-World of Relations
- Finding and Connecting with your Spirit Guide
- Memory Divination for the Formative Years
- The Imprints of Conception and the Visions of the Soul
- The Tree of Self-Unfoldment

Each of the three workshops also includes a number of yogic-alchemical light-fire practices, designed to clear the perception channels, for the divinations. Participants who successfully complete all three workshops obtain a Certificate of Completion.

Please consult the website: www.metzneralchemicaldivination.org, for details.

Metzner Alchemical Divination® is a registered trademark.